"*God's Not Done With You* is bot how God rescues, restores, and ways. In an era when hope a these stories will inspire you to greater faith in the God who has great plans for your life!"

ROBERT JEFFRESS, Pastor, First Baptist Church of Dallas, Texas

"What the world needs now is *hope*! In this book, John Meador shows us that it is never too late for a new beginning: that one setback doesn't make a failure. We get to bat again. Read it... and reap!"

O.S. HAWKINS, Best-selling Author, *The Promise Code*

"What a great book! Reading it reminded me of my own story of setback, and the similar stories of many who I pastor. This book will be a wonderful encouragement and blessing for those for whom confusion or pain is loud, and who need to hear that God's not done with them."

STEVE ROBINSON, Senior Pastor, Cornerstone Liverpool, UK; Director, Acts 29 UK

"John Meador knows something about struggles and facing great odds. Robbed of his hearing as a young boy as a result of illness, he does not even hear himself speak, yet he has mastered the art of preaching without hearing even his own voice. His own struggle makes it natural for him to speak up for those who are facing various challenges in their lives. The pages before you will encourage you, thrill you, challenge you, and confront you with your own need for a second chance in life. God is not through with you yet!"

JIMMY DRAPER, President Emeritus, LifeWay

"I'm already making my list of loved ones to send copies of this book to. The comeback stories from the Bible apply so aptly to crises they're facing: depression, disobedience, disillusionment, difficult people to deal with, debilitating health challenges... Here is a direct, inspiring message from an authentic voice."

DIANNA BOOHER, Author, *Lead With Confidence!* and *Communicate Like a Leader*

"The Bible is not only a book to believe but also to be lived. This is the reason why so much of God's word is written in the very human stories of real people. John Meador delivers the stories of men and women like you and me who step from the pages of Scripture to show us how to overcome and live in hope every day. We all enjoy comeback stories, and *God's Not Done With You* is a great read for those who want to keep going and never quit as we face life's challenges. If you want more grit and more grace in your life, this book is for you!"

JACK GRAHAM, Pastor, Prestonwood Baptist Church, Plano, Texas

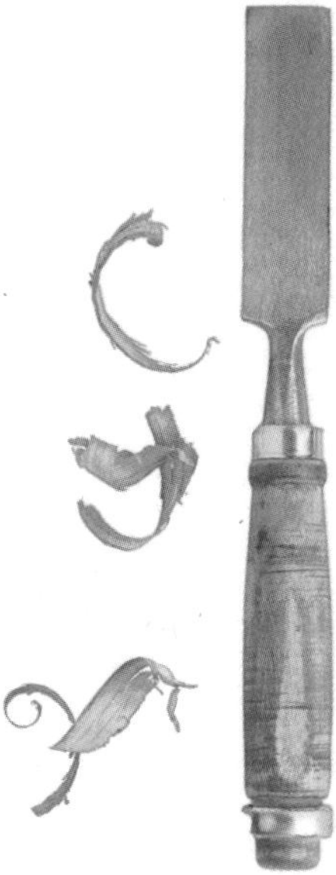

GOD'S NOT DONE WITH YOU

thegoodbook COMPANY

To my wife, Kim.

Your authentic faith, tireless dedication to passing faith on to our children, and encouragement to me to be faithful to the Word in preaching and writing have consistently buoyed me.

What a blessing you are!

God's Not Done With You

Published by:
The Good Book Company

thegoodbook.com | thegoodbook.co.uk
thegoodbook.com.au | thegoodbook.co.nz | thegoodbook.co.in

Emphasis added is the author's own.

ISBN: 9781784988654 | Printed in Turkey

Cover design by Drew McCall

Contents

Introduction

Wherever you are, no matter what has happened to you, God is not done.

I write this introduction from Cabo San Lucas, where my wife and I are staying on a brief retreat gifted to us by friends. The Sea of Cortez is gorgeous, and on this day, sizable waves are crashing into the steep portion of a beach where we are walking, just next to a jagged outcrop of rock. It's a dangerously beautiful place to stand in, and I am fascinated by the ebb and flow of the ocean—the rising of the waves and the loud crashing of the water on the rocks, then washing back into the sea, only to do it over and over again.

It looks a bit like life, with its daily rise and fall of circumstances, slow recovery, and then the challenge of another day and different dilemmas. Life, they say, ebbs and flows.

On this day, however, my beach experience is a bit more complicated. While capturing a video of those waves from a sandy portion of the beach just next to the rocks, I am surprised by an enormous rogue wave that crashes completely over me. Its force knocks me off my feet and pulls me down the steep drop into the sea. Holding tightly to the phone I've been using to film the waves, I fight my way back to my feet and scramble to safety just before the next wave comes crashing in.

The video I was able to capture, by the way, is awesome. I escaped unscathed but lost a bit of my pride and one of my favorite beach sandals.

In life too, rogue waves surprise us and knock us off our feet. Challenging setbacks in life are far more difficult to navigate than rogue waves—and they sometimes cost us things we never intended to surrender.

Your own challenges in life may look more like tsunamis than isolated rogue waves: seasons when it seems impossible to find anything to hold onto at all and nearly unthinkable to come back from. And yet, comebacks *are* possible from the most devastating situations imaginable. Countless stories are told of these incredible rebounds and rescues—whole books devoted to the minute details of these dramatic battles for life and meaning.

I know these sorts of stories because I have walked some of them myself and have for many years walked with others on these journeys.

People struggling with loss and disappointment.

People who've encountered sudden tragedy and search to try and make sense of it.

Friends who battle through serious physical illness and who wonder what the outcome will be.

Stories of those who ask questions about where God is when these things happen.

Stories that also ask, "Am I done? Is God finished with me? Do I still have purpose?"

I've set my mind to find an answer to those questions. And I promise you, when we make that search, God is to be found in our suffering.

No book tells these stories more powerfully than the Bible. In character after character, thrilling and inspiring comeback stories of Scripture give hope and encouragement. The accounts contained in the Bible are unique in contrast with all other great stories in that they reveal the narrative of the God of the universe, who masterfully brings every needed resource to the comeback operations in our lives. He's the God who is forever redeeming our past to give us a future.

Maybe your life is simpler. Perhaps you've not yet experienced agonizing defeat and discouragement. I assure you, in time you will, and what is written within will be worth reading.

On the other hand, maybe you're skeptical. Your life may feel more like the massive tsunami than the rogue wave, and you wonder if idealistic-sounding Bible stories can really inspire or instruct you. I urge you to keep reading, for these stories are about real-life events that often brought more drama, more heartbreak, and more tragedy, with more at stake than most any other situations in history. They show us greater and more meaningful outcomes than we can possibly imagine.

There is the story, for example, of a leader who committed the most public and embarrassing act of adultery in history and arranged a deadly, shameful cover-up of his sin. But somehow, God was not finished with him. Or the surprising account of a woman who was the wife of an irrational fool who taunted armed warriors. While her husband's act of defiance nearly brought on the slaughter of his entire household, God rescued her out of that desperate situation, and then elevated her to an entirely new position. Just when she felt life was over, it wasn't!

Nine amazing stories—nine real-life scenarios that give us hope for our own comeback seasons. There are common themes in these stories that I am eager for you to read—truths that are absent from every other type of rescue scenario. Transcending the predictable narratives where someone overcomes hardship through simple grit, these tell of unbelievable changes of heart and circumstance, and the presence of One who makes all things work together for your good. These are God-sized stories, and here are the seven truths you'll find woven throughout them:

1. God is intimately involved with the details of our lives as we go through rogue waves and tsunamis—even when we're not aware of His involvement.
2. In your worst hours, you are not alone. He is the God who is *there* with you. He is *for* you.
3. God gives promises to ordinary individuals and keeps them. It is those fulfilled promises that change outcomes.
4. He has made amazing resources available to us in our most trying moments that are only for those who trust Him in the battle.
5. God will teach us the art of how not to self-destruct while we're waiting on answers and solutions.
6. He provides a divine grace that empowers us to persevere—a resilience that enables us to get up again and trust that we will make it through because He is never finished with us.
7. God will use your difficult circumstances to build trust in Him, forge strong character in you, and show others the power of God working within your situations.

I promise to help you discover how these truths work, where they are found, and when you can expect great moments of breakthrough. While God works in mysterious ways, He also reveals those ways to those who seek Him. This book leads you to those ways, and by reading, you are seeking. There's a promise in Scripture that he or she who seeks shall find (Luke 11:10).

These truths are not simply *taught*, as in a classroom, but *caught* in real-life situations—perhaps the exact kind of situation you are presently facing. It's in real life where faith meets doubt and where we experience the fulfillment of His plan and purpose—even in the most trying times.

Read all these stories. You'll need them all. God has recorded the details of these lives so that we might know about them and learn from them. He's shown us these stories because He wants you to see Him more clearly in your own life and your own challenges.

In this season of your life, whatever it may be, get caught up with me in the greatest victories of all time and bring them by faith into your own life and the lives of those around you.

You are going to learn that *God is not done with you*.

Chapter 1

Your Past Need Not Define You

MOSES' STORY

"God saw the sons of Israel, and God took notice."

Exodus 2:25

In recent years, a young man named Brad has moved from the periphery into the mainstream of my life and work. One day I asked Brad an innocent question: "Where were you when I moved here?"

His answer: "In jail with my father."

Now, that's a reply that makes you want to dig deeper. And I did. I learned that Brad had been brought back from a painful past. Raised in a home with turmoil and abuse, he was brought to faith by a believing mother but did a lot of running—from home, from church, and from faith. He also ran from the law. He was so in and out of trouble that it took him two years to complete his senior year of high school, and there wasn't much promise of improvement ahead. One night he was arrested, along with his father, during a family dispute—and together they went to jail.

Over time, he began to turn back toward a relationship with God. He told me, "I felt like I was called to something greater," but he had no idea what that was. His was a gradual journey, and within a few years, Brad learned that he had never escaped the attention of God. Today, he finds himself processing the past and is amazed that God has worked so powerfully to bring him back.

Brad is the worship pastor of the church I lead—and it's remarkable to see what God is doing with this young, growing leader who impacts thousands of people through ministry.

That's a long way from "in jail with my father."

Brad's story is one of many that demonstrates that God can orchestrate an extraordinary comeback from a difficult past—and that even when times are dark, He is not done with us yet.

And then there's Moses, whose story is an epic account of a troubled past. Storytellers have been fascinated by who he was and what he experienced. He was the rescuer of a nation. A leader of perhaps millions. Mental images come to mind of a historic leader with a flowing beard, holding his hands out over the seas as they split apart. He's on the mountain, holding tablets that God Himself has inscribed with commandments—glowing with a glorious countenance as he descends from the pinnacle. If there was an Old Testament superhero, this is the guy.

Countless books have been written and movies made of key seasons of his life. Few, however, focus on *the dark part* of his life.

Moses' life is most clearly understood through three 40-year seasons. The first season is told in a mere 15 verses of Exodus 2. It's the story of his birth, miraculous rescue from certain death as an infant, and unlikely adoption into the house of Pharaoh—the ruler of all of Egypt. Moses' life is one of privilege and passion, with a deep love for his nation, Israel—a nation in bondage to Pharaoh.

His sense of justice for his people stirs his anger when he sees one of his fellow Israelites beaten, and he kills the Egyptian oppressor. Now Pharaoh is angry and tries to capture Moses in order to put *him* to death. Moses flees 360 miles into the desert region of Midian (a 20-day journey) in order to escape. This first period of his life ends with these words:

> *"But Moses fled from the presence of Pharaoh and settled in the land of Midian, and he sat down by a well."*
> *(Exodus 2:15)*

Fifteen verses. Forty years. A meteoric rise with unprecedented opportunity. A tragic, compulsive decision to take another's life, and then an escape into exile in order to avoid capture and execution. This begins the second season of his life, the dark one. This is the portion of Moses' life that no movies are made about. It's the quiet, dark period where fear is all-consuming and past actions are regretted. Far from the place of his family and people, he's a long way from his destiny. He's on the backside of the desert of his life. It's a tough place to be for anyone, and especially this one, who has lost so much.

Human nature and personal experience lead me to believe that Moses is living in the land of regret and sorrow. Surely, he's aware of his amazing rescue from the death sentence proclaimed by Pharaoh over all the male Hebrew babies born around the time of his birth. How could he not know of his unique privilege and opportunity—to be trained in the royal palace and have extraordinary influence as a young man? It was an incredible place to be—a divine placement from which he might have spoken on behalf of his people.

Yet, in spite of all that God had done to place Moses in such a place, one swift action of angry personal revenge brought it all down—and with it the opportunity of a lifetime. He's far from where God placed him and far from family and friends. Alongside that comes the mental beratement and self-condemnation Moses must have experienced on his escape to Midian. We know Moses to have been a passionate man. We know he experienced the gamut of emotions in his lifetime. Many tears fell in that desert.

Grief and regret from something we've done bring overwhelming sorrow when we realize what has been lost. Most of us have been there in some way. I remember standing at my mother's grave years ago and being completely overwhelmed at what was lost—what would never be—after she lost her battle with cancer. I didn't cause it, but I felt it to my core.

Moses had *caused* this loss. He recklessly and angrily took matters into his own hands and destroyed the life of another man—and along with it, his own future. From his perspective, what was lost would be forever lost. In his mind, there was no comeback scenario. It's in this kind of situation that we wonder if God knows or even cares about where we are anymore. After all, no one else does.

Anger Can Ruin, but God Can Rescue

As a teenager and later as a young adult, anger nearly ruined me. It wasn't the "Moses level" of anger, but it was frightening.

I thought my anger was due to what others said or did to me—when something was said behind my back or I was ridiculed in front of others. Being rejected by those I most wanted acceptance from would set me off. Failing to perform in a sports event would send me into a tantrum.

Anger began to invade my everyday life like a fog moving in—a darkness that seemed to be out of my control. I lost friends and a roommate; I broke bones in my hands from hitting things in frustration.

On the worst night of my young adult life, I raced my car down a highway, angry at life and bitter about the outcomes, looking in desperation for a place at which to aim my car and end my life. Thankfully, I ran out of courage, and the moment passed. I will never forget just how close I came to ending it that night.

For many, a moment like that doesn't pass easily. People often pay a high price for what they have said and done in angry moments.

Moses, one of history's greatest leaders, nearly forfeited an entire future because of his anger.

But God had a way of rescuing Moses—and He has a way of rescuing us.

God was not through with Moses, but Moses had no idea. At times, our faith is as good as dead before God raises it up again.

Have you ever run from your past? I love that the Bible gives us so many examples of people, who, like ourselves, have something to hide.

Adam and Eve tried to hide their original sin from God in the garden.

Abraham and Sarah laughed at God's promise while trying to hide their deep doubt.

David had an affair with Bathsheba and tried to hide it by arranging her husband's death.

These are just a few examples of actions that caused incredible grief and undeniable damage, yet God covered Adam's sin, blessed Abraham and Sarah with a son, and restored David's kingdom. God is famous for bringing people back from the dead—figuratively *and* literally.

When God Is Not Done

God often, and famously says, *I'm not done with you yet!*

But how does God do that? How did He bring purpose back to Moses?

It took time. Lots of time. If the first 40 years of Moses' life are detailed in the first 15 verses of Exodus 2, the next 40 happen in the last eight verses of the same chapter. Moses has an encounter with the seven daughters of Reuel, the priest of Midian, that eventually leads to his marriage to one of those daughters, Zipporah, and the beginning of their family. Moses is truly a stranger in his heart and mind to these people, but he puts down roots in that very different place.

He's living life on the backside of the desert, pasturing a flock of sheep for his father-in-law, far removed from the God of his fathers and far from his former life. And with no hope—or thought—of return.

A lot can happen in 40 years. We can lose sight of where we came from. Over 40 years of time, we can grow distant from even remembering the God who rescued us. We can forget His powerful promises. Our hearts can grow calloused, and our faith can become as good as dead. Even our loved ones can become just a distant memory, like a chapter of a book long forgotten.

And in those 40 years, the plight of the sons of Israel back in Egypt grew only worse. But...

> *"God saw the sons of Israel, and God took notice of them."*
> *(Exodus 2:25)*

God also saw Moses, and when it was time, God began a new season with this man, starting right where he was, near a mountain in the wilderness.

God meets us where we are. Isn't that an encouraging thought? It's especially encouraging if we're in a situation we don't want to be in, and of which we have no idea how to get out—but God knows. And *He takes notice*.

New Seasons of Life Begin with New Encounters with God

I believe that God still arranges encounters with us. I believe from my own experience, but more importantly for historical reasons. The Bible is filled with examples of God encountering men and women in embarrassing places and revealing Himself in powerful ways. In the first book of the Bible, we read about the first man and first woman (Adam and Eve), who had rebelled against God and were hiding from Him. God found them, and spoke to them, and it seems ultimately led them to be restored to relationship with Him and able to carry out His significant plans for their lives! (See Genesis 4:1, 25-26.)

Moses' encounter, as with most of us, involved **listening to God**. As you read this book, you'll be reminded that God spoke to people in history in unmistakable ways. You'll also learn that He speaks to us in the present day through the Scriptures and His Holy Spirit, and by how He answers prayers and meets needs. He still speaks. Over the years, I've been strongly influenced by Francis Schaeffer's book, *He Is There and He Is Not Silent* (Tyndale House, 1972). The title alone challenged my thinking as a young man. What Schaeffer writes about in a philosophical way has practical implications. God speaks!

If God speaks, we must also be listening *for* Him and *to* Him. I'm convinced that's the biggest challenge. God speaks but, for a variety of reasons, we're often not listening.

Moses, most likely, had not heard from God in more than 40 years. Not since that ill-fated attempt to take matters into his own hands and murder the Egyptian.

Not since his own countryman mocked him the following day, having discovered the crime. Not since he fled the presence of Egypt and found himself far from everything.

And then one day, **God gets Moses' attention** and speaks. It's interesting to me that Moses is pasturing a flock of smelly sheep in the wilderness that he doesn't even own. He was the "most likely to succeed" of his generation, but look at him now. As Moses comes to a mountain rising up out of that desert, he has no idea his life is about to change. We know the mountain as Horeb, also known as Sinai, and in the record of Exodus 3, we read that this is the "mountain of God" (v 1). It later becomes the site of other with God. Only God can take an insignificant old mountain and turn it into a place where life is forever changed.

> *"The angel of the LORD appeared to him in a blazing fire from the midst of a bush; and he looked, and behold, the bush was burning with fire, yet the bush was not being consumed." (Exodus 3:2)*

It's an unusual way to get someone's attention, right? God can call to us anytime, anyplace and in any way, and He sometimes uses the unusual. So, here is an angel appearing to Moses in the midst of this fiery bush. It stops him in his tracks. "I must turn aside now and see this marvelous sight, why the bush is not burning up" (Exodus 3:3). While it's *all* phenomenal, the emphasis of Scripture is that it gets Moses' attention. He's ready to listen!

> *"When the LORD saw that he turned aside to look, God called to him." (v 4)*

Moses is stunned but unharmed. He's near the fire but not in the fire. He's unable to explain what is happening, but he's listening. God often works this way. It may possibly be where He has you at this moment!

Notice what's happening with Moses:

He is ALONE with God. This is not the only time when Moses is alone with God, but it's a prerequisite for hearing God clearly. In our world today, it's difficult for most of us to be alone without distraction. But honestly, God has our attention best when we are all alone. Cherish solitude as a time when God can speak to you. Build quietness into the margins of your life and into the rhythms of your day-to-day. My best times with God have been times alone with God.

He is LISTENING to God. God will often speak to us in times that are circumstantially difficult. For example, at crossroads in life where we don't know what to do, He can direct us. In tragedy and heartbreak, He can give us grace for that day and the next. In sickness or disappointment, God is ready to speak to us and often will. Tough times might just *be* your burning bush.

He is READY. Moses' words were few: "Here I am" (Exodus 3:4). I'm a talker. I have too many words too often. However, when I sense God speaking, I'm ready to listen. *Here I am* is a great way to begin—and continue—to listen to God.

He is HUMBLE. There are many attitudes that I can envision for a man who has been herding sheep on the backside of the desert for 40 years, but being prideful is not one of them. An absence of pride places him in the best possible position to clearly hear and obey God—as a humble man. Moses has no solutions of his own. He has no plans to pursue. God is looking for just that kind of person. The Bible later declares, "God is opposed to the proud, but gives grace to the humble" (James 4:6). Humility looks good on all of us. It especially looks good to God, who never fails to pour out His grace to us when we need Him the most.

It may well be that this work of humility was the greatest single thing Moses needed. It may be what God does for you to get you ready for His next assignment. It certainly was for me—and untold numbers of others. It's a great, refining fire in our soul. Like the fire in the bush, the purifying fires of humility burn away our pride but preserve us intact for God's "next" in our lives.

Moses is listening. God has his attention. In Exodus 3, God begins to speak in ways that help us know His purpose, and here it is: God is speaking so that Moses can know Him. God wants all of us to truly, personally, and intimately—*know Him*.

How Well Do You Know God?

New seasons begin when we know God well enough to allow Him to lead us. Until we know Him, and until we know His power and ability, we will never see beyond our checkered past. We will not be able to see how to move forward and, most importantly, who will move us forward until we know more about the God who calls us to a new season.

Moses certainly knew God in a general way. He knew the stories, the history, and the past experiences of God's people. He knew the creation account, the life of Abraham, and was fully acquainted with how God used Joseph to preserve the nation of Israel. He knew why they were in Egypt, but he didn't understand how or why or when God would rescue the people who seemed forgotten. He may have prayed but had probably lost hope that God had heard. That's what makes someone take matters into their own hands—they don't know where God is or what He's doing. Moses needed to *experience* God.

So God introduces Himself to Moses. He begins by having Moses remove his sandals from his feet, "for the place on which you are standing is holy ground" (Exodus

3:5). It's as though God is saying, "You're in a unique moment, Moses. I'm going to reveal Myself to you. Get ready for this. I am the one and only God, who is meeting you." Can you imagine this moment? Have you ever been there? Are you willing to go to that kind of place?

> *"**I am** the God of your father—the God of Abraham, the God of Isaac, and the God of Jacob." (v 6)*

This caused Moses to hide his face "for he was afraid to look at God." It wasn't a moment of shame or guilt. It was the moment of recognition. In Scripture, this title—"*I am* the God of Abraham, Isaac, and Jacob"—could only describe the one Creator God. The one who is eternal. Moses knew this was God Almighty. Any encounter with this God is the encounter of a lifetime.

> *"I have certainly seen the oppression of My people who are in Egypt ... I am aware of their sufferings." (v 7)*

Had Moses continued to pray for Israel? Had he for 40 years wondered whether God was watching or aware of the desperation of Israel? Had he cried out over and over? If he had, here's the answer to those prayers from God. *I know. I'm aware. I've seen.* It is human nature to doubt God, but here is God's answer for Moses—and His answer for you.

> *"So I have come down to deliver them from the power of the Egyptians, and to bring them up ... to a good and spacious land." (v 8)*

While there is much more detail in God's words and promises to Moses and Israel, the point is clear: God has heard the prayers, and He is coming.

And does He ever. Moses is about to know God better than He ever dreamed. He'll be used by God in ways that completely overwhelm his past and his own understanding. But first, He must *know God intimately*.

Moses was at the conclusion of his season of darkness. The burning-bush experience brought light to more than that mountainside. He was getting ready to break through to a new season that would be illuminated by his encounter with God.

Before Great Things Happen, We Must Believe God

The end goal of every true encounter we have with God is that we can ultimately trust Him with our lives. That's what allows us to believe God is not done with us. We must trust Him enough to walk in a new direction, and to believe Him for new assignments. Here was Moses' new direction:

> *"And now come, and I will send you to Pharaoh, so that you may bring My people, the sons of Israel, out of Egypt." (Exodus 3:10)*

God was going to walk Moses back all the way to Egypt, back to the brick-making bondage of Israel, back to the palace of Pharaoh, and God was going to deliver His people as only *He* could. God often makes us walk back before we walk forward. We may have to walk back to the scene of our departure. It may be the place of sadness or hurt—where we must somehow go back and forgive. It could be the place of rebellion and self-will. It may well be the place of an unfinished work of God in your life, as it was with Moses.

If I were in Moses' shoes, I'd be remembering the failure at the first attempt. There's a lot in that baggage. But I'd also be remembering, even louder than that, the words I have just heard from God. Listen to them above all.

The next 30 verses are an incredible dialogue between Moses and God. You should read this section yourself. It's a crystal-clear illustration of how we struggle to believe God when He leads us. Moses has a stream of objections.

"Who am I, that I should go to Pharaoh?" (v 11)

"What shall I say to them [Israel]?" (v 13)

"What if they will not believe me or listen to what I say?" (4:1)

"Please, Lord, I have never been eloquent!" (v 10)

For each objection, God has an answer. When I read these objections, I remember so many of my own crises of faith in following God. And I remember that He always has the answer.

It is not until the latter part of Exodus 4 that we read:

"Then Moses departed and returned to his father-in-law Jethro, and said to him, 'Please, let me go, that I may return to my brothers who are in Egypt.'" (v 18)

God has changed Moses. He has convinced Moses that he will never be alone again. Moses, on his part, has become willing to do whatever God asks. When God's "I AM" becomes our "I will," amazing things happen. You must believe God's game plan is far better than yours ever was. Like Tony Evans says, "You can't have Jr. Varsity faith for Super Bowl victory." Of course, we all know this about a sporting event. It's even more true about life.

God has also changed others during this time. Israel is now ready. Moses' accusers and critics are now gone. Egypt is now ripe. It's time to come back.

Once Moses obeyed and took the first step back to Egypt from Midian, he began the amazing journey of overcoming his past. God was with him every step of the way through the confrontation with Pharaoh, through the plagues and the deliverance and exodus of God's people—all the way through the Red Sea and back to the mountain where the fiery bush got his attention and the Lord called Moses to Himself.

God seems to remind people that He's not done with them yet. He does it with people that we might call prominent, and He does it with those we would call ordinary, but he begins by calling us back from dark and obscure places. Whether it's a Brad or a Moses, God *takes notice* of us and calls us to something greater.

For Saul, it happened on a road to Damascus, when he heard, "Saul, why are you persecuting Me?" (Acts 9:5). For Peter, it took place after his denial of Christ, when Jesus said, "Peter, do you love Me? ... Tend My sheep" (John 21:17).

For me, the moment took place when God calmly and gently urged me to continue, despite my confusion, anger and pain. *I'm not done yet. Your story isn't over*, He said.

Is it time for your comeback? Is there some portion of your life you must overcome? Is there some season that needs to be reversed, so that you can listen, hear, and believe God again?

Earlier, I asked you to imagine the moment Moses had with God. Now I ask you to dwell on what God might say to you here and now, and to consider how you might respond.

Perhaps God is at this moment whispering to you, *I am not finished with you. Let's continue our journey together.*

Chapter 2

The 50/20 Principle

JOSEPH'S STORY

*"You meant evil against me,
but God meant it for good."*

Genesis 50:20

We've all known people who seemed to face extraordinary adversity. For many, one catastrophic event marks their life for many years. Others experience difficult circumstances in waves. Nothing seems to work out for them. They nearly always end up disappointed, and those around them are perplexed as to why it's happening.

Jeff and Diane (not their real names) are *those* people. Jeff was brought up in a highly dysfunctional, abusive home. He was to struggle for decades in various ways as a result of that abuse. Diane came into his life, and they began their family and faith journey with high hopes and determination. They had the typical challenges of a young family, but even an outside observer could tell that these challenges were much greater, deeper, and more frequent than most. Adversity never seemed far away. Though multitalented, Jeff struggled to find his niche in his life's work. Doors that should have been open were frustratingly slammed shut when he approached.

Jeff and Diane would experience brief seasons when life began to be stable; then circumstances would change suddenly, and they would have to start over. While Jeff was rising in one career, false accusations were brought against him, and although the resulting investigation proved him innocent, he still lost his job. They attempted a new start in another city, but unexpected and severe health issues sidetracked them. These kinds of things became a pattern for their lives.

Now in their 50s and on the other side of the health setbacks, Jeff and Diane are still looking for the right open door and are working through still more challenging circumstances. Somehow, they keep moving forward. They still believe that God is directing and protecting them. Watching them persevere is inspirational. It's enough to make one ask, "What's the secret to such confident trust?"

How do they handle the tough, unspoken questions, like *Where is God when things rarely seem to work out? How do I know He's a good God?*

Everyone faces occasional adversity and challenging circumstances. We are relieved to weather them quickly and look for life to get back to normal. But what if those tough times are not brief or limited? What are we supposed to believe about life when we face *constant* adversity?

Knowing God Is Not Done with You

Sometimes life really is hard, and the stages and chapters seem never-ending. Sometimes adversity gets worse, not better. Sometimes pain increases.

The story of Joseph is perhaps the greatest story of encouragement in the entire Bible for those of us who struggle. Joseph's life is detailed in the first book of the

Bible, and nearly 14 chapters are devoted to his life and experiences.

At the *end* of this long story, Joseph makes an incredible statement about God's sovereign power and reveals a secret that we can build our life upon:

> *"You meant evil against me, but God meant it for good."*
> *(Genesis 50:20)*

I call this the 50/20 factor. It becomes apparent in the endgame for Joseph's life. The 50/20 factor is a simple reminder that regardless of what our life looks like as we move forward, we will one day look back and see how God has used it in a meaningful way. It's not 20/20 vision; it's 50/20.

There's an important reason to tell Joseph's familiar story by beginning... at the end. What God was going to do for Joseph in the end, He's promised to do for others. In fact, it's extremely important for you to see *your* story from the same end point.

Think about it: beginning at the end helps us put people and circumstances in perspective. Not everyone who opposes us is ultimately our enemy. Not every setback in life is tragic. Not every false accusation is without purpose, in the end. But, in the moment, we have no way of seeing all this pain redemptively apart from knowing the end.

This approach also helps us remember that God is always working, even when we can't see the evidence for that. It helps me know there is purpose in life's adversity and trials, and while I can't trust the person/circumstance causing me problems, there is One I can trust. This is a reminder to believe in the existence and working of the sovereign God, who will in the end clarify how all things will work together. Simply put, this approach helps us walk by faith.

When You Experience Rejection

Now, the beginning...

From early on in life, Joseph faced **the adversity of rejection**. Most people tell the story of Joseph by focusing on the "coat of many colors" and the favor Joseph enjoyed from his father, Jacob, but there's a deeper, more painful picture that dominates.

Joseph's family had grown in a way that created strife on many levels. His mother, Rachel, died giving birth to his younger brother, Benjamin. Before they were born, their father, Jacob, had already fathered ten sons. When you read the family story in Genesis 29 – 30, you see the details of possibly the most dysfunctional family in Scripture.

The Bible makes it clear that Jacob favored Joseph, giving him a special coat:

> *"Now Israel [Jacob] loved Joseph more than all his other sons, because he was the son of his old age; and he made him a multicolored tunic." (Genesis 37:3)*

Favoritism is an unhealthy complication in any family, but especially this one.

> *"His brothers saw that their father loved him more than all his brothers; and so they hated him and could not speak to him on friendly terms." (v 4)*

Can you imagine Joseph wearing that coat in front of his jealous brothers? Joseph was a young teenager at this point and was not aware of what was unfolding around him in the family. His love for the coat given to him by his father (along with the obvious favor he enjoyed) triggered increasing animosity. Then we read this:

> *"Then Joseph had a dream, and when he told it to his brothers, they hated him even more." (v 5)*

Joseph's dream of his brothers and father bowing down to him was like adding a spark to the kindling set for fire. In the end, these dreams would become significant and prophetic, but they were despised when shared. His brothers hated him even more with an intense jealousy, and even his father rebuked him.

Jacob decides to send Joseph to find his brothers, working as shepherds in the fields, and bring word back to him about their well-being. As Joseph approaches, the brothers see him coming—and still seething in jealousy, they create a plan.

> *"When they saw him from a distance, and before he came closer to them, they plotted against him to put him to death." (v 18)*

His oldest brother, Reuben, manages to intervene, but what happens next brings Joseph face to face with intense, hateful rejection.

> *"They stripped Joseph of his tunic, the multicolored tunic that was on him; and they took him and threw him into the pit." (v 23-24)*

Imagine yourself in Joseph's shoes. He's despised, hated, plotted against, and left in a pit by men who hate him. And this is his family! His fate is about to be determined by ten angry men—a terrifying prospect.

Together, they decide his fate. He's to become a slave—sold to Midianite traders who happened by at precisely that moment.

For the next twelve days, Joseph made the laborious trip to Egypt, wondering with every step what had gone wrong and what would become of his life. Rejection does that to a person. It can make us replay our life through a dark lens.

Rejection sinks deep into our souls. It threatens to destroy what we think about ourselves, our value, and our future. Rejection in our lives can happen because we're different, or just because we're not part of an accepted group. Our appearance or actions may factor into rejection. Our skin color or background may trigger it. What we've said or done can cause it.

More than those factors, however, the cruelty and insensitivity of others is a huge part of this story. Joseph's brothers were jealous—filled with hatred and envious of his favor.

I can remember a season in life when I felt intense rejection, and it wasn't my imagination or insecurity. It was real. I recall the introspection, the doubting of myself and of the purpose for my existence. For some reason, I always thought I was to blame—and then one day I realized it wasn't really about me. It was about others.

The rejection I felt from others had been completely misinterpreted. God had not rejected me—only others. My own personal battle against rejection was settled in a parking lot on my college campus while I was seated in my car one evening, crying out to God in my misery. I was at the end of myself, or at least I thought I was.

In that moment, I heard from God—a memorable moment, when God spoke to me in a way that I'll never forget. As He often seems to do with me, God impressed a simple question on my heart, and here's what it was.

I accept you. Is that not enough?

That's all I *heard*, and it required an answer. I knew God wanted me to respond. In that long, holy silence, I became aware of a new truth. I needed to trust Him for this. My answer was *Yes, God, You are enough*.

I'd already settled the question in my heart that Jesus Christ was my Lord and Savior. My faith and trust in Him for salvation had taken place years before. I knew the gospel: the good news that God loved us unconditionally and sent Jesus to die on a cross to pay for our sin. I'd already made the decision to trust in Jesus for my salvation, but I understood it to be primarily about eternity. On that night, in that parking lot, the reality and power of His forgiveness and unconditional acceptance hit home to me in the most relevant *here-and-now* way. I came to know His acceptance and favor in a daily way—completely undeserved—and I learned to walk in that confidence. It changed me.

From that moment on, certain verses began to resonate in my heart—truths which transformed my own image of myself. I began to believe that I (and others who come to Christ) am blessed...

> *"... with every spiritual blessing ... He chose us in Him ... He predestined us to adoption ... In Him we have redemption ... the forgiveness of our wrongdoings, according to the riches of His grace which He lavished on us." (Ephesians 1:3-8)*

That experience became a defining moment of my life. I learned that it is God's acceptance and love that we really need, and He offers it freely. Have you had that moment?

When Others Reject You, God Does Not

We're not given a glimpse of Joseph's faith during this season of his life, but we can see it once he gets to Egypt. There he shows a devotion to God and an independence from the opinions and whims of others that convinces me that he trusted God—even when he experienced painful rejection from others.

Without that trust, we can't move forward—especially when difficulties keep coming.

When Your Character Is Slandered

Joseph's next challenge is one of **false accusation.**

When Joseph is sold in Egypt to a high-ranking member of the bodyguard of Pharaoh, a man named Potiphar, something unexpected happens. Joseph's descent from favored son to household servant is followed by a rapid rise in respect and favor in his new surroundings.

> *"The LORD was with Joseph, so he became a successful man. And he was in the house of his master, the Egyptian." (Genesis 39:2)*

Repetition in Scripture always calls attention to something significant. In this case, one phrase is repeated four times in Genesis 39. It's so encouraging! "The Lord was with Joseph." After the rejection, loneliness, and solitude he had experienced, this statement places hope in the heart. If God is with you, is that not enough?

Potiphar notices what he's got in Joseph, so he makes Joseph an overseer in his household.

But someone else has noticed Joseph—Potiphar's wife. She sees this young man, filled with youth and favor, and she's noticed his availability. Plus, as the Bible puts it, "now Joseph was handsome in form and appearance" (Genesis 39:6).

Potiphar's wife sees him and wants him for herself. She's bold and persistent with her seduction, but Joseph knows he must be faithful to God and to Potiphar. One day, she sees a perfect opportunity with no one else nearby. She grabs his garment and demands that he comply. He refuses again and flees, leaving his garment in her hands. Furious, she immediately begins making false accusations against Joseph.

In spite of Joseph doing everything right, this doesn't end well. Life sometimes produces agonizing injustice.

Adversity doesn't happen just because we do wrong things. It can happen because we do the *right* things, and what we do (or refuse to do) goes against the grain of the people and culture around us. It can happen when we don't fit the narrative or the expectations others have for us. Joseph does everything right, but it all goes wrong, and Potiphar imprisons him.

Potiphar's wife means it for evil against Joseph. She's punishing him. Now Joseph is an enslaved foreigner, accused by a leading woman of attempted rape. He's immediately judged as guilty and imprisoned.

What happens to Joseph is unfair in every way.

False accusations demoralize us. They stun us and halt us in any forward movement we're making in life. They destroy our reputation and cause us to doubt the existence of justice. They make us wonder how God—who knows and sees all—could allow it to happen. We ask, "Where is God?" And yet, here it is again—that incredible touch of grace:

> *"But the LORD was with Joseph and extended kindness to him, and gave him favor in the sight of the warden of the prison." (v 21)*

When Others Believe The Worst about You, God Stands with You

When we read through Joseph's chapter of false accusation, we see God affirming him when no one else would do it—by His presence. The chief jailer found Joseph to be as loyal in jail as he had been in Potiphar's house, and Joseph was elevated again.

But Joseph's life *still* remained difficult. You wonder, "When will this end?"

Sometimes in life we have the same question, don't we? *When will this season of my life change? When will my sickness be over? When will my livelihood be restored? When will my family be restored? When will God hear my prayer?*

We ask a lot of questions about *when*, mainly because we're not good at waiting.

Joseph did a lot of waiting. He was in Potiphar's house for eleven years before being sentenced to prison. And now, he's been in prison long enough to gain the trust of the head jailer and become a confidant among the prisoners. Two notable servants of the king of Egypt, a cupbearer and a baker, were confined during Joseph's time in prison.

Isolation and Loneliness

This sets the background for another disappointing time for Joseph—**the adversity of isolation**. He's going to be forgotten and is going to wonder if anyone knows where he is.

Have you ever wondered if even God knew where you were? I remember years ago talking with an amazing couple in church ministry who served in a remote area of the United States. When our church hosted them in a conference, the wife expressed herself in such an open way. She said, "How did you find us? Sometimes I wonder if even God knows where we are." If we're honest, we wonder the same thing at times.

God, where are you? If you're there—if you're aware of what I'm going through—show me! Say something! Do something!

Was Joseph thinking this way? We certainly couldn't blame him if he was.

So, Joseph has quickly gone from being well known in the house of Potiphar to being just another prisoner.. When the two prisoners from the king's palace have disturbing dreams, they are downcast and disturbed. Joseph notices, and they share their dreams with him.

Joseph interprets the dreams, and, amazingly, the interpretations come true. The baker is put to death. The cupbearer is restored to the powerful king of Egypt, which could turn out to be a breakthrough for Joseph.

"Yet the chief cupbearer did not remember Joseph, but forgot him." (Genesis 40:23)

Is there anything worse than being forgotten and being left alone, wondering, "Is my life over? Is God finished with me?"

These are the life chapters in which the psalmists and the prophets say, *How long, O LORD?* This is where we wonder if God knows where we are and what we're going through.

"How long, LORD? Will You forget me forever?
How long will You hide Your face from me?
How long am I to feel anxious in my soul,
With grief in my heart all the day?" (Psalm 13:1-2)

God Knows Exactly Where You Are

Have you seen the computer program called Google Earth? It has a mesmerizing feature that allows you to zoom in to a specific spot on the planet and see the details of that area. Someone used this feature to show a close-up picture of an individual sitting in a beautiful field. From there, we can see the camera zoom out until we lose focus on the individual but are able see an incredible view of the sphere of the earth, and then the planets and solar system. It's an interesting way to look at the universe. It's also enlightening to realize how small one person is in our gigantic world. It reminds me of how easy it is to be forgotten in the sea of humanity.

However, if you reverse the feature to zoom back in to the original spot, you watch the universe recede into the background, and the focus becomes the same individual in a beautiful field.

What Google Earth does with technology, God does every single second of our lives. He sees us and doesn't lose us in the vastness of His creation. He knows exactly where we are. He can and does zoom in on the details of our life moment by moment, even when we are not aware of it.

Sometimes we need these kinds of reminders.

God sees you and knows where you are: "Your heavenly Father knows" (Matthew 6:32).

While you are waiting, God is working: "Teach me ... Lead me ... For You I wait" (Psalm 25:4-5).

One day you'll look back and realize He never abandoned you. "I will never desert you" (Hebrews 13:5).

When It Seems You Are Completely Forgotten, God Knows and Remembers

If we know the end of Joseph's story, we know that God was preparing him for incredible and incomprehensible moments in the days ahead. Joseph had no idea. And in our lives, neither do we.

Sometimes we must simply wait.

English Anglican minister and author, Nicky Gumbel, said it this way, "Who you become while you are waiting is as important as what you are waiting for."

Joseph's journey had been treacherous and painful. None of the people in his life proved trustworthy—only God. If you're going to be like Joseph, you must loosen your grip of confidence in people and strengthen your grip on God.

And now, we're coming back to the end. We started at the end—with the 50/20 principle.

"You meant evil against me, but God meant it for good."
(Genesis 50:20)

The Final, Climactic Chapter

One day, while Joseph is waiting, the ruler in his palace has disturbing dreams that no one can interpret, and the cupbearer suddenly remembers Joseph and tells Pharaoh about him, who wastes no time summoning him.

Pharaoh tells Joseph the dreams, and God shows Joseph what they mean. There will be seven years of plenty followed by seven years of famine. Joseph further tells Pharaoh to look for a man to set over Egypt to prepare for this unprecedented event. So Pharaoh makes a decree:

> *"Since God has informed you of all this, there is no one as discerning and wise as you are. You shall be in charge of my house, and all my people shall be obedient to you; only regarding the throne will I be greater than you."*
>
> *(Genesis 41:39-40)*

Let this sink in. Pharaoh has taken a rejected, solitary foreigner in Egypt, who has been previously imprisoned for supposedly assaulting an official's wife, and he has installed him as second-in-command of Egypt! No doubt he's been impressed by the wisdom and favor God has given Joseph, but it's still a stunning choice.

Now Joseph is in a leadership role in Egypt, and Genesis 41 – 50 will show us that God fulfilled His revelation through the dreams to the exact detail. The prophesied famine created an opportunity for Joseph to forgive his brothers for what they'd done to him and to restore his family. From there, God used Joseph to actually save them from perishing and to secure the future of Jacob and the nation of Israel.

Only God could have made this possible, and He did it through the life, hardships, and character of Joseph, which unfolded through many years. God wasn't done with Joseph!

Character matters. Integrity protects. Perseverance rewards. Joseph's character is demonstrated with astounding clarity through dark circumstances. God uses it all.

Without Joseph's rejection, he would not have been sold into bondage to traders.

Without an arduous twelve-day journey he would not have arrived in Egypt.

Without the false accusation, he would not have spent time in prison.

Without the prison, he would never have met the cupbearer.

Without the cupbearer, he would not have been called by Pharaoh.

Without the presence of God, he would never have made it through any of this.

It's all tied together.

This is where the 50/20 principle is so clearly stated. This is the verse you'll keep coming back to.

> *"As for you, you meant evil against me, but God meant if for good in order to bring about this present result, to keep many people alive." (Genesis 50:20)*

In the New Testament, we read a companion verse to this truth.

> *"And we know that God causes all things to work together for good to those who love God, to those who are called according to His purpose." (Romans 8:28)*

In The Sovereignty Of God, Even Acts of Evil Serve His Ultimate Good

Christopher Ash—in an article at desiringGod.org entitled "Who Causes Your Suffering?"—poses a great question:

> *"How do we think about the sovereignty of God in a world where Satan and evil exist? On the one hand, we may neglect Satan altogether and just assume that God rules the world in a simple and direct way (that God is responsible for sin and evil). On the other hand, we may think of Satan (or sin) as a second, independent autonomous power of evil, in which case the universe becomes a terrifyingly uncertain place, since we may never be sure whether God or Satan will win any particular round of their contest."*

Of course, neither of these is true. God, in His sovereignty, is able to harness the actions of evil men and direct them to a divine purpose. Satan and evil are also subservient to the purposes of God in our lives. The greatest example in history of this is the cross of Christ, where humanity's wickedness in crucifying Jesus was part of God's predetermined purpose to rescue humanity through the sacrifice of His Son (see Acts 2:22-24). What people meant for evil, God used for good.

If God could work the complicated elements of Joseph's story for good, He can do the same for you. If God could be trusted to get Joseph through the bitterness of rejection, the injustice of false accusation, and the loneliness of being forgotten, can He not also be trusted by you?

Derek Redmond is a name I'll never forget. A 400-meter British Olympian sprinter, he held the British record for this race and won gold medals in two World Championships. At the Olympic Games in Barcelona in 1992, he was running at top speed in the semi-final race when his hamstring tore, rendering him unable to continue. Yet, he refused to quit. Though the other sprinters had long crossed the finish line, Derek Redmond agonizingly and painfully attempted to finish the race himself, limping and hopping a few yards at a time. The cameras and the crowd shifted their attention from the finish line to the incredible sight of a man who was unwilling to give up on his race.

Suddenly the cameras focused on another man—an older man who'd jumped the barriers between the crowd and track, pushed his way past security guards, and made his way alongside Derek Redmond. We learned later that this man was his father, and together they crossed the finish line to a standing ovation. I can't watch this video without emotion.

I don't remember who won the 400-meter Olympic gold medal in Barcelona that year. I do, however, remember the man who ran the most painful and, in many ways, the most noble race that day: Derek Redmond.

Derek was the man who finished the race because of his grit. And because of his father.

That's how you'll finish your race. With the grit that comes from trusting and growing through adversity. And with your father—your heavenly Father.

Chapter 3

God Gives Real Hope

ESTHER'S STORY

"... and if I perish, I perish."

Esther 4:16

Despair is something nearly everyone knows about. The dictionary defines despair as a loss of hope—as a mindset that gives up any hope of something better happening in a circumstance, a season, or a life. Despair can drive us to furious effort in an attempt to change things, or it can render us passive—just awaiting the inevitable end.

Despair and hopelessness are where we are if we think God is done with us. We usually arrive here because nothing in life is making sense. Our circumstances are not working together, and we're growing weary. But if you're still here, *God is not done with you yet*. If you find that hard to believe, let me introduce you to a woman named Esther.

The story of Esther in the Bible is riveting. Comprising just ten chapters, it tells the astonishing story of a woman who experiences hopelessness on several levels. Hers is a world of pagan culture, repressive patriarchy, murderous racism, and drunken revelry. When you first start reading this story, you'll soon be wondering, "How did she get here, and how will this end?" Everything seems to be going against her.

Her citizenship was hopeless. She was a stranger in the land where she lived. Esther's ancestors had been taken into exile from Jerusalem, her home, to Babylon during the 70-year Babylonian Captivity (605–536 BC). When Babylon was defeated by King Cyrus of Persia, the Jews were released to go home, but Esther's family stayed in Babylon. They were in a minority and held no influence. If anything, their lives were daily threatened, especially, we learn, by one of the most wicked men in Scripture, a man named Haman. He hated the Jews and was determined to exterminate them—and he had the influence to carry his plan out.

The culture in which Esther lived was hopeless. The opening chapter details the life of King Ahasuerus. Everything in this first chapter sets the scene for corruption at the highest levels. We're introduced to an enormous, national banquet thrown by the king. The party is filled with egotistical pride on display, drunken debauchery, and corrupt sexuality. As this event moves to a climax, the king makes the lewd request that his beautiful queen dance before these drunken men. The banquet actually ends with Queen Vashti, a courageous woman, doing the unthinkable and refusing Ahasuerus' request. This leads to an angry series of meetings and edicts from the king demanding the removal of Vashti and requiring women in the land to honor any requests their husbands might make of them. It is completely disastrous.

On top of that, Ahasuerus' counselors determine that a nationwide search for Vashti's successor will commence immediately. Esther would be one of the young virgins selected to go through the grueling year-long process of becoming either the queen or just another member of the king's harem. There were no other choices. It was in no way an enviable position.

Her circumstances seemed hopeless. In the background of this narrative is the tragic story of Esther's loss and loneliness in the death of her parents. It's clear that this young woman has suffered much in her life; however, her adoption by her uncle, Mordecai, who turns out to be a strong and protective influence for her, provides guidance for her in all she encounters.

Esther's circumstances were so extreme that we might struggle to identify with all she encountered—and there are few stories that compare with hers. But then we look around us at the world we live in and say, "No, I see hopelessness where I live as well." Our hopelessness may not take on the characteristics or the degree of Esther's situation, but it is there.

What If We Cannot See Hope OR God?

Hopelessness has set in when we no longer believe a situation can be redeemed. Despair results when we lose faith in God—as well as in people—because we see no evidence that He is aware of our pain and heartbreak. Hopelessness is obvious when we stop praying, stop looking for God's hand at work, and stop thinking about how anything can be different.

Humanity hasn't come far since Esther's day. Hopelessness is still around.

But so is God. And God is never done with us.

The book of Esther is unusual and different from all other books in Scripture in that it never mentions the name of God (though Song of Solomon mentions it only once, in 8:6). There is no record in this book of God communicating with Esther, Mordecai, or anyone else, even though we see Him speaking with many others throughout other parts of Scripture. We don't see God sending angels to help in the book of Esther. He doesn't part seas or do anything that seems physically impossible that we know of.

What we're left with is a series of implausible circumstances and coincidences that end extraordinarily well for Esther and Israel, *or* we are left with an amazing depiction of the God who works unseen and unheard, and with sovereign, supernatural precision to redeem those He loves. He's rarely early but never late. He places people and scenarios together as in an amazing tapestry being woven, which makes no sense from our side but complete sense on the other side. He uses the ordinary faithfulness of dedicated people to bring about an astounding deliverance of great significance.

These kinds of things bring real hope to otherwise hopeless situations in life. The Bible uses the word "hope" in a unique way. Hope for us is a wish or a dream. "I hope things work out," we say in wishful hope. It's an optimistic mindset that wants good things to come. It is synonymous with staying positive.

Scripture, on the other hand, uses the word "hope" to describe *confidence*. It is the desire of some good with the expectation of obtaining it. In Romans 5, Paul gives great practical wisdom about how trials (and hopelessness) work to bring hope.

> *"And not only this, but we also celebrate in our tribulations, knowing that tribulation brings about perseverance; and perseverance, proven character; and proven character, hope; and hope does not disappoint, because the love of God has been poured out within our hearts through the Holy Spirit who was given to us."*
>
> *(Romans 5:3-5)*

It is God who gives us that hope. He gives us the confidence to move forward and hope to hold on, and enables us to trust Him as Esther did, to work everything out in the end.

Finding Hope by Finding God in the Compassion of His People

Here's what we learn about hope from the life of Esther.

We find hope to hold on when His compassion is expressed. One of the major story lines in this book concerns the action and heart of a great man: Mordecai. It is this man—in a culture of prideful, wicked, sinful people—who shows Esther extraordinary compassion and care. In doing so, Mordecai reminds Esther of the kind of God she loves and serves.

Before we meet Esther, we hear about Mordecai.

> *"There was a Jew at the citadel in Susa whose name was Mordecai ... He was the guardian to Hadassah, that is Esther, his uncle's daughter, for she had no father or mother. Now the young woman was beautiful of form and face, and when her father and her mother died, Mordecai took her as his own daughter."* (Esther 2:5, 7)

This is an unusual adoption in trying times. Esther is not in his immediate family. Mordecai could have ignored her and tended to his own circumstances. He could have simply sent her away. Or, in keeping with the pagan culture around him, he could have married her and kept her for himself. Instead, he shows compassion, without which there would be no story.

Mordecai, a man obviously devoted to God and His ways, demonstrates compassion toward Esther, and that brings her hope that God Himself knows her need.

Compassion describes the character of God.

The psalmist said:

> *"Remember, Lord, Your compassion and Your faithfulness,*
> *For they have been from of old." (Psalm 25:6)*

Nehemiah's prayer, spoken just a few years before Esther's day, recognized God's compassion in allowing Israel to return from exile.

> *"Nevertheless, in Your great compassion You did not make an end of them or abandon them, for You are a gracious and compassionate God." (Nehemiah 9:31)*

This was not lost on Esther. In fact, this brought about unusual devotion and loyalty in her life toward Mordecai. She listened to him and trusted him. She sought his counsel in the most difficult of times. Each time she reached out—he was there. It's amazing how compassionate people can bring hope!

Jesus was filled with compassion. Scripture teaches that Jesus was *moved by* compassion, *felt* compassion for people, and *had compassion* on the multitudes. Compassion reflects the heart of God and says loudly to us that we can have hope in hopeless times because of who God is.

A mentor of mine, Spiros Zodhiates, often said, "Compassion wins every time."

Ultimately it was the compassion of God that rescued Israel through the supernatural events that were unfolding in Mordecai's and Esther's lives, and it is the compassion of God that led Jesus to a cross 2,500 years later to rescue mankind from the bondage of sin and death.

In a world of hopelessness, you and I can represent God's compassion—and we should. And if you're in a hopeless situation, look around you for someone somewhere that will remind you that God knows, cares, and will have compassion on you when you need it the most. He is there. He is aware. He does care.

As I look back on life, I've realized that God has been faithful to place certain people around me who brought encouragement to me and dedicated prayer for my life. He sent people who reminded me that *they* had confidence that God was going to come through and provide answers. Often, it was the presence of these kind of people that reminded me of God's goodness and faithfulness, and who helped me look ahead in faith. Do you see people like that nearby? They may not announce their arrival, and they may not even realize *why* they are in your life—but my experience is that they are there.

Finding Hope by Remembering God's Way

We can also find hope to hold on when we remember that God redeems tragedy. Before Esther *lived* this story, she *knew* this story. As a Jewish girl raised first by her parents and then by the righteous man Mordecai, she knew well the story of the redeeming God, who rescues His people. The Jewish people were known for their dedication to passing on the stories of their faith in Almighty God. As we will see, Esther shows every evidence of knowing who has gone before her:

- Abraham and Sarai believed God for a son, Isaac, and God birthed the nation of Israel through him.
- Moses was rescued from a criminal past and became the deliverer of Israel from Egypt.
- Deborah, the warrior and judge, rescued Israel from a certain defeat.
- David, the shepherd boy, rescued Israel by slaying Goliath, and became king.

- Daniel and his friends were rescued from perils such as hungry lions and a fiery furnace.
- Nehemiah was released from his service to the king of Persia to return to his land and rebuild Jerusalem's walls.

God is a redeeming God who uses ordinary men and women to rescue those He loves. As a Jew, Esther would have known this story. She must have recalled the vivid details of such an incredible history. Maybe she wondered what her place would be in redeeming the present distress of her life and the threat to her nation.

Certainly, Mordecai wondered. At a critical moment, he said to Esther:

> *"And who knows whether you have not attained royalty for such a time as this?" (Esther 4:14)*

If hope is the confidence and certainty of a good outcome, no matter how desperate the situation looks, doesn't the evidence of the God who has worked in history give us hope? The writer of Hebrews says so:

> *"Now faith is the certainty of things hoped for, a proof of things not seen. For by it the people of old gained approval." (Hebrews 11:1-2)*

We don't see how God is at work, but we believe it. We may have reasons to doubt, but we have bigger reasons to hope. God has done it before, and He can do it again. It is the very nature and pattern of God's character to redeem tragedy and bring back situations from hopelessness and defeat. Hold on to your hope in *that*.

Even more than these, we can hold on to hope in God's sovereignty. If God is indeed God, then He is in complete control, and nothing is without purpose. This is true of your life as much as it was of the lives of Esther and Mordecai. Job says it well at the end of his time of trials:

> *"I know that You can do all things,*
> *And that no plan is impossible for You."* (Job 42:2)

Remember the choice we must make in how to approach the book of Esther?

We must either admit to a series of incredible coincidences, confirmed by historical documents, or we must choose to believe that God indeed *does* work everything together for His purpose in a sovereign way. If it's the former, good luck. If it's the latter—we have hope!

Countless are the times I've had to remind myself of this. Every time a door was shut that I believed needed to be opened—an opportunity shut down that seemed important—I've had to go back and remind myself that God is at work and is aware of where He has me. He's never off the throne, and never does He take His eye off my situation.

Here's the unfolding of the story. Esther is selected to audition for the king and finds favor with Hegai, who was in charge of the women. After a process of many months of preparation and beautification, each of the selected women would spend a night with the king. Esther found favor in the eyes of all those she encountered, and ultimately she found favor with the king.

> *"The king loved Esther more than all the women, and she found favor and kindness with him more than all the virgins, so that he set the royal turban on her head and made her queen in place of Vashti."* (Esther 2:17)

During this time, Mordecai discovered a plot against the king and, being a righteous man, reported it to Queen Esther, who told the king. It was investigated and confirmed, and Mordecai's good deed was recorded in the king's book of history.

Stay with me here for this chain of events. The king appointed wicked Haman, who hated the Jews, to a role of great authority, and Haman began to plot. Ultimately, Haman despised Mordecai the Jew and planned his execution by building gallows on his own property. In addition, he convinced the king that the Jewish people as a whole were a threat and secured an edict that would allow the people of the kingdom to slaughter the Jews on an appointed day. Esther learned of this and was in great anguish, while Mordecai counseled her to speak to the king in order to save the Jews.

It is at this point that Esther and Mordecai have a conversation that is as famous as any in the Bible.

> *"If you keep silent at this time, liberation and rescue will arise for the Jews from another place, and you and your father's house will perish. And who knows whether you have not attained royalty for such a time as this?"* (4:14)

Here is the hope of Mordecai on display. He trusts in the God who redeems and rescues. He knows God will come through but is unsure of how it will happen.

I love this mindset of Mordecai. There is no doubt he's desperate. He knows what is at stake. He also knows God has not spoken yet, and that the final outcome has not taken place. If you and I can live with this attitude and this trust in God, hopelessness can never really capture us completely.

Esther, on her part, agrees:

> *"Go, assemble all the Jews who are found in Susa, and fast for me ... And then I will go in to the king, which is not in accordance with the law; and if I perish, I perish."* (v 16)

This is Esther's admission of hopelessness *and* hope. *It seems hopeless*, she says, *but I place my life in the hands of the sovereign God. If He allows me to die, so be it.* It's a serious moment and a serious commitment.

Hopelessness and hope live next door to each other. Often we waver between the two.

"Good and evil run on parallel tracks," said the preacher Ron Dunn, "and they arrive at about the same time." I couldn't agree more!

Esther seems to understand this and is transparent about the risks and the threat. But she is also resolved to trust God—or die trying.

She plans a banquet to meet with the king and Haman.

What happens next defies the boundaries of normal circumstance. But for the sake of illustrating how supernatural this event is, allow me to describe it as many others have, with the language of coincidence.

It *just happens* that the king chooses Esther, a Jew, out of hundreds of beautiful young women to be his queen. This *just happens* to take place at the exact time when Haman is plotting to kill the Jews, and especially Mordecai. It *just happens* that Esther asks for a banquet with the king and Haman, and as they meet, she asks them to meet again the next day. It *just happens* that on the night before the second banquet, the king cannot sleep and asks his servant to read to him from the archives; and the servant *just happens* to read of the noble deed of Mordecai in informing the palace of the earlier plot kill the king—a deed that has gone unrewarded. It *just happens* that all this transpires at the exact moment when Haman walks into the court and the king asks Haman how he should reward Mordecai. This creates complete agony in Haman's life, who *just happens* on that day to have built gallows on his estate that he intends to hang Mordecai upon.

At the banquet, Esther exposes Haman to the king, and the angry king asks Esther what should be done. It *just happens* that one of the king's men knows of the gallows that Haman has *built* and offers that as a solution. The king says, "Hang him" (7:9), and Haman dies on the gallows he's built for Mordecai.

The result is that Mordecai, Esther, and the Jewish people are saved. The story moves from chaos and certain tragedy to order and victory for God's people—from hopelessness to great hope and confidence in God.

Stretch Your Faith

This series of events is fascinating to me. Maybe I've simply seen God do too many things that align perfectly in multiple ways in answer to prayer to believe any of this could be simple coincidence. Or perhaps I'm just not naive enough to believe it was done without God.

Is it such a stretch to believe that the God who spoke all of creation into existence can also intervene in our own lives with precision and power? Is it too far-fetched to consider that His interest in Mordecai and Esther is the norm and not the exception? Is the God who declares the end from the beginning, and who knows all that is between those two points of time, unaware and uncaring of our own dilemmas?

Not according to Jesus. He made sure His disciples understood this truth:

> *"Are two sparrows not sold for an assarion [like a cent]? And yet not one of them will fall to the ground apart from your Father. But even the hairs of your head are all counted. So do not fear; you are more valuable than a great number of sparrows." (Matthew 10:29-31)*

This, of course, is the passage that gave inspiration to a famous hymn which has brought reassurance to so many over the years: "His Eye Is on the Sparrow." These are the lyrics of the third verse:

Whenever I am tempted, whenever clouds arise,
When songs give place to sighing, when hope within me dies,
I draw the closer to Him, from care He sets me free;
His eye is on the sparrow, and I know He watches me;
His eye is on the sparrow, and I know He watches me.
(Civilla D. Martin, 1905)

I cannot imagine what areas of hopelessness you may be facing, but there is a God in heaven who knows these things about you. His eye is on the sparrow, and I know He watches you.

The message of the book of Esther is unmistakable. God is there, even when you cannot see Him and even though you may not hear from Him. He is working everything according to the counsel of His will, and He doesn't miss a detail or waste a moment.

It's my personal conviction that this book is placed in the Bible to give us hope and freedom from the despair that we often feel. It's here to remind us that even when you do not see God's direct actions, or visibly see His intervention for you, He is still working "all things in accordance with the plan of His will" (Ephesians 1:11).

When you hold on to hope because of your confidence and trust in what He has done in the lives of others, you will one day look back with far more understanding and appreciation for the hard times He's allowed *you* to walk through.

You'll have your own story and conviction that God is not done with you yet.

Chapter 4

Saying Yes to God

JONAH'S STORY

"But Jonah got up to flee to Tarshish from the presence of the LORD."

Jonah 1:3

Angela is a woman with a vibrant and strong faith. For more than a decade, I've known her and her husband and see them on a regular basis. After I mentioned the prophet Jonah and his season of disobedience in a conversation she was a part of, Angela told me her own story.

Years ago, Angela's first husband died, and she entered into a time of grief mixed with anger. Struggling to deal with her loss, she lost her spiritual bearings and began to associate with a very different group of people from her Christian brothers and sisters. With the encouragement of her new friends, she made one decision after another that put her on a path of willful disobedience against God. Step by step she grew further away.

Angela was running from God.

On one hand Angela still professed faith, but her actions were plainly disobedient to all He called her to. She told me, "My heart was far, far from God, and I didn't care."

Angela's story is quite common. Often, I hear a similar narrative to the one she told me. Biblically speaking, I believe one can be a true believer but wander.

"Prone to wander, Lord, I feel it / Prone to leave the God I love," is part of a beloved old hymn that many know by heart (Robert Robinson, 1758). We know it because we've occasionally lived it.

We Are Prone to Wander

Even prophets have wandered away from God. Jonah comes to mind. His story begins with reluctance, selfishness, disobedience, and desperation. This prophet is a picture of how we often run from God.

When I was in high school, the principal arranged for a horrifically wrecked car to be placed near our school entrance to show us the worst-case scenario of bad driving. The message was clear: *Don't take driving lightly.* I've never forgotten it.

Jonah is a man displayed for us to stare at—like that wrecked vehicle—and be warned by because of the disastrous place in which he landed in life. The message is: *Don't take obedience lightly.*

But the story doesn't end there. Jonah finds the love, persistence, and patience of the God who cannot be outrun. The story of Jonah is why I stopped running from God, and he's why you should stop too.

Jonah's story opens with God giving Jonah **a specific command to obey**. There is no preface, introduction, or preparation for what we're about to read. It starts with God speaking to Jonah.

> *"The word of the LORD came to Jonah the son of Amittai, saying, "Arise, go to Nineveh, the great city,*

and cry out against it, because their wickedness has come up before Me." (Jonah 1:1-2)

The big story here is that God is the One who communicates to men and women, who then make choices and respond. Some people run to God. Others run away. Still others live in bewilderment as to why life has become so confusing and adversarial, when the reason might simply be that they are living in disobedience.

God has a plan for this world and for your life. It's a plan centered on him saving His people through faith in Christ and bringing everything under the rule of Christ (see Ephesians 1:7-12). It's an amazing plan, but we're not often aware of how it all fits together. God communicates His plan for His people and the world through the Scriptures to reveal truth and calls us in a personal way to respond to His love *and* His commands.

His commands help us know how to live, how to relate to each other, and how to respond to circumstances. His commands help us leave behind destructive things and move toward constructive things. They build character and discipline and love and goodness in us. They help us walk in alignment with God, the Creator of the universe.

And sometimes we don't want to obey them. So, we disobey God.

Pride Pulls Us Downward

It only takes a single verse to reveal Jonah's **proud response**.

"But Jonah got up to flee..." (Jonah 1:3)

Jonah knew what God had in mind. He knew God wanted to show compassion on people that Jonah didn't particularly like. At the end of his story, Jonah makes this admission:

"I knew that You are a gracious and compassionate God,

slow to anger and abundant in mercy, and One who relents of disaster." (4:2)

Jonah didn't like the people of Nineveh or the plan God had. He didn't want to do what God called him to do, so he decided to take matters into his own hands. He openly resisted the command of the living God. Believe it or not, that's a serious thing.

"But Jonah rose up to flee to Tarshish from the presence of the LORD. So he went down to Joppa, found a ship which was going to Tarshish, paid the fare and went down into it to go with them to Tarshish from the presence of the LORD." (1:3, NASB95)

Every word of this verse paints the picture of disobedience in a life. God has a plan, *but* we decide to do something different. Jonah rose up to flee *from the presence* of the Lord. He wanted to go to the city of Tarshish, which was as far as he could get from where God had sent him—2,500 miles in the opposite direction. He went *down* to Joppa, *down* into the ship, and paid the fare himself, and that decision took him far from God's favor.

Can you sense the general direction that Jonah is heading in? He's always moving *away* from God. He's always going *down*. He's also *paying for this* himself. You'd think that at some point Jonah would realize that this was a losing battle, but he refuses to acknowledge it.

Pride and stubbornness are twin evils. They egg each other on.

When Angela described her time of wandering, it sounded eerily like Jonah's going down into the ship and sailing far away from God into a sea of storms. Disobedience—*any* disobedience—is taking matters into our own hands and doing what we want to do, regardless of the price we'll pay.

Remember the first sin, where Adam and Eve directly and proudly disobeyed God's command by eating forbidden fruit? God's command was for their protection, but their disobedience took them into danger and death. They ran from the presence and favor of the Lord.

It's an age-old but relevant line that says, "Sin will take you further than you want to go, keep you longer than you want to stay, and cost you more than you want to pay." Most of us have felt that at one time or another. It's a terrible place in which to be, whether we admit it or not.

God's Response to Pride

Disobedience and pride have an even greater consequence, though. The result of pride and disobedience is that we are set against God's nature and character.

> *"God is opposed to the proud but gives grace to the humble." (James 4:6)*

God *will always* oppose our pride. It's his nature. He's not being adversarial—we are. It doesn't make sense to want to be opposite God—to be on the other team against God. But that's where Jonah was. It's also where Angela was at a certain time in her life. Maybe that's where you've been before—or where you are now. It's just what happens when we say no instead of yes to God.

What happens next in Jonah's life is something you should know.

Jonah's disobedience brings **painful lessons**.

It doesn't take long for God to respond to Jonah's disobedience. That's not always the case, but it certainly is here. Just two verses into the book of Jonah, we begin to see what God is going to do and how He is going to oppose Jonah's pride. In fact, the remainder of this book of four chapters details God's response to a single act of disobedience.

I've often summarized what God did here in Jonah's life, and it always sounds a bit bizarre, but here it is: God sent a storm and a fish, He raised up a plant and a worm, and then He blew a scorching wind against Jonah—all of it designed to get Jonah's heart and obedience. This tells me that God is going to use big things and small things, the natural and the supernatural—all couched in our context—all designed to get us to face Him.

And when all those things are *opposed* to us and our disobedience, we learn what it feels like for God to be "opposed to the proud."

I'm not a sailor, but I've been at sea in a ship in a storm. Fifty miles off the coast of South Texas in the Gulf of Mexico, deep-sea fishing with 90 other men on a large fishing boat, we ran into a squall that brought high winds and waves. I remember seeing nothing but sea for a few seconds while watching the bow of the ship plunge into the wave, and then seeing nothing but sky in the next few seconds as it rose up and pointed skyward. A few minutes of this, and nearly every person on board was hanging over the rail, emptying our stomachs into the ocean. It was miserable.

Jonah's trip was worse: **God sent a storm.**

> *"The LORD hurled a great wind on the sea and there was a great storm on the sea, so that the ship was about to break up." (Jonah 1:4)*

It was a *great wind,* and there was a *great storm,* so that the ship was about to *break up* (v 4). It was more than miserable. Even the seasoned sailors were afraid and began to jettison the cargo, as they realized the boat wouldn't hold together for long (v 5).

What makes this storm worse is shown by the wording we see at the beginning of its description. "The Lord hurled a great wind..." This is not just a squall or a sudden windstorm.

This is a God-storm. This is God opposing the pride of Jonah. This is God saying, *You may think you're going to Tarshish, but you're not going to get there.* Not every storm we experience is a God-storm in that sense, but this one was.

What stuns me about this storm is not the immensity of it or the timing of it. What shocks me is the fact that every sailor on board is desperate and concerned for their life—while Jonah is asleep in the hold of the ship (v 5). They are looking for someone who can tell them how to call upon *any* god to rescue them (v 6). Jonah, on the other hand, is doing his stubborn best to ignore it all.

It's amazing to me that lost men—rough, hardened, pagan sailors who know nothing about the God of heaven and earth—can ask the real prophet in the boat, "How could you do this?" (v 10). In other words, *How could you disobey the living God and then involve us?* It's a fair question. Jonah's disobedience has put them all in the path of apparent destruction.

The Price of Pride around Us

Pride has many innocent victims. Pride in one person brings misery to many. The people that are unfortunate enough to be close to us when we run from God will suffer by their proximity to us. Poor moral choices implicate others around us in the worst possible ways. Did Eve's choice to disobey God in the garden affect Adam (Genesis 3:6)? Of course it did! Together, Adam and Eve's disobedience affected the entirety of mankind.

In a more direct way, Jesus warns us about stumbling blocks—actions that make others take disobedience lightly along with us.

> *"Woe to the person through whom the stumbling block comes!" (Matthew 18:7)*

Disobedience doesn't stay in its own lane. It wanders and crashes head-on into innocent travelers on a different journey.

Jonah knew the answer to the dilemma: "Pick me up and hurl me into the sea. Then the sea will become calm for you, because I know that on account of me this great storm has come upon you" (v 12). Reluctantly, the sailors did, and the sea "stopped its raging" (v 15).

Now the men in the boat are worshiping, and Jonah is sinking.

What happens next is incredible.

God appointed a fish. This terminology is not my own; this is the record of Scripture.

> *"And the LORD appointed a great fish to swallow Jonah, and Jonah was in the stomach of the fish three days and three nights." (Jonah 1:17, NASB95)*

Do you believe in miracles? There are at least three miracles happening here, and while they may stretch our limited imagination, they are no less true for that.

It's a miracle that God creates a fish so large that it can swallow a man whole. It's a miracle that He can communicate with this large fish to swim to the precise part of the sea where it can swallow a prophet. It's also a miracle that Jonah is able to come to his senses while in the belly of the fish and cry out to God.

Skeptical? Think about it with me. This is the same God who parted the seas at the perfect time to rescue His people from Pharaoh. He made the sun stand still for a day to allow Israel's victory in war (Joshua 10:12-14). He speaks, and the invisible wind blows the leaves on a thousand trees—it shouldn't be hard to believe God would perform miracles to call a person to repentance.

It's hard to imagine what Jonah experienced in the fish, but there are stories in history that reveal what it may have been like. In recent times, a Cape Cod fisherman off the coast of Massachusetts was swallowed by a humpback whale but quickly spat out, surviving with only minor injuries.

Another incredible account was of a man named James Bartley, swallowed by a sperm whale off the coast of the Falkland Islands in 1891 and presumed dead for 36 hours until the whale was harpooned and skinned, and Bartley was discovered still alive in the belly of the whale. His skin was bleached, and he was blinded by the gastric juices, but he lived another 18 years to tell his story. His tombstone reads, "A Modern Jonah."

In the biblical account, we learn that Jonah's experience took place in the Mediterranean Sea, where the *average* depth is one mile (5,180'/1,579m), and the deepest part is more than 3 miles. He was a long way from air, from hope, and from God. Before being swallowed by the fish and while sinking in the water, he remembered that "the deep flowed around me ... seaweed was wrapped around my head" (2:5). Sounds like the bottom to me—the very bottom.

Whatever the physical effects may have been for Jonah of being in the depths and in the belly of a great fish, the part of this terrifying experience most mystifying to me was the timing of Jonah's final surrender. He waited to the very end before asking for deliverance. Why do we so often wait until the last moment? How much more evidence do we need to be convinced that we've messed up?

At that moment, I'm sure Jonah was convinced that God was done with him, but he was wrong again. Still, he cried out to God one more time.

"While I was fainting away,
I remembered the LORD,
And my prayer came to You,
Into Your holy temple." (Jonah 2:7)

It was then that the Lord commanded the fish, and it vomited Jonah up onto the dry land after he had spent three days in its belly.

Surrender Sooner Rather Than Later

It would have been much easier to simply say yes the first time. We all know this to some degree, I think, but we're prone to wander. It's a hard and frequent lesson I must learn in my own life.

The storm, the sea, and the fish were difficult things for Jonah to bear. God's responses to disobedience are hard. But they are also filled with grace, favor, and the goodness of God.

It was grace because God stopped Jonah from going *further* away from His presence.

It was grace because God brought him *back* to the starting point.

It was grace because God was still going to *save* the Ninevites.

It's all grace. The fish was grace. The pain Jonah experienced was grace.

But most of all, it's grace that God hears our desperate cry, regardless of how far we are from him, or how deep the depths that we've descended into. Even three miles deep.

King David knew about these things.

"Where can I go from Your Spirit?
Or where can I flee from Your presence? ...
If I dwell in the remotest part of the sea,
Even there Your hand will lead me,
And Your right hand will take hold of me."

(Psalm 139:7-10)

We almost never see the storms that hit us in times of disobedience as grace or favor. We rarely view the whales and circumstances that swallow our lives to be grace. Pain and suffering are our enemies, we think. I can remember being *so* angry at God during times of painful and frustrating heartbreak—when situations seemed unbearable—and yet it was the pain that brought me to the place of being desperate for God.

When pain and suffering bring us back to God, they are our very best friends. They make us see things in a different light. They make us look to God when we otherwise would not.

Jonah, now in Nineveh, hears the Word of the Lord a second time, and he takes the simplest path—he just obeys. "So Jonah got up and went" (Jonah 3:3). It's far less complicated than any other response we can give God.

Like Jonah, for you to say yes to God involves saying no to your first tendencies. The writer of Proverbs helps us here.

> *"Trust in the LORD with all your heart,*
> *And do not lean on your own understanding."*
> *(Proverbs 3:5)*

This verse has often rescued me from a well-intentioned but wrong response to God. It can also deliver us from an intentional disobedience.

This verse in Proverbs has helped me recover from many "no's" in my life because it has helped me understand *why* I sometimes said no. I simply thought I had a better way! We never have a better way or a better plan than God!

Remember how this chapter began with the story of Angela? Her return to God involved a dream that alarmed her, a conversation with someone who had been praying for her, and the encouragement of a spiritual mentor who told her to pour her heart, her anger and her pain out to God. God used all those to bring her back to Him.

When Angela came back from disobedience, she *really* came back. She's one of the most passionate worshipers I know—and it is completely authentic. Her heart has come back to Him.

God might not send a storm or a great fish, as he did with Jonah. He might not use dreams or visions as He did with Angela. God has many other elements at His disposal to get your attention—and He shows us a couple of those when Jonah becomes reluctant *again*.

Surrender Your Whole Heart

Jonah obeyed and God used him in great ways in the wicked city of Nineveh, but Jonah was still miserable and angry. This time his issue was not one of disobeying a direct command but hatred in his heart for people who were not of his nation or race. He obeyed God on the outside but not on the inside. He was harboring major issues, and *this* may have been the biggest problem in Jonah's life.

So what was Jonah's response to this great outpouring of God's love for Nineveh?

> *"Please LORD, was this not what I said when I was still in my own country? Therefore in anticipation of this I fled to Tarshish, since I knew that You are a gracious and compassionate God ... So now, LORD, please take my life from me." (Jonah 4:2-3)*

Most of us have experienced it: we do the right thing but hate it all the way. We don't want favor to be shown to people we don't like. We struggle with those who don't look like us or act like us, or who in some way have hurt and offended us. We're still harboring a selfish and sinful heart, and God won't leave it alone.

This is where plants, worms, and winds come in. These are the little things that grate against our souls. Like the gritty pieces of sand and stone in our shoes that blister our skin till it bleeds, the irritations we face rub us raw until we decide to do something about them.

God raises up a plant, a worm, and a wind. Jonah sits down outside the city to see what will happen. No doubt he's worn out from his running away, being cast overboard and being swallowed by a great fish. He's weary from the three-day journey of obedience and from preaching all day long in an intimidating city.

So God raises up a plant, and Jonah is suddenly "overjoyed about the plant" (v 6). The next day God appoints a worm to attack the plant and make it wither. Then God sends the wind to scorch Jonah again, and now Jonah is ready to die again.

How is it that everything in creation seems to obey God, except man? The storm, the waves, the fish—all respond immediately to their Creator. The plant, the worm, and the wind—the same. Only Jonah says no. Only mankind has been given a free will—and we dare to exercise it against the better wisdom of our Creator.

The message from this interesting string of events is clear. Jonah only loves himself. He only cares about what God does for him. He has no concern for the great city of 120,000 people that God so graciously saved. He's not ultimately concerned about fully obeying God.

A Lesson and a Surprise

The final words of the book are both a lesson and a surprise.

> *"Then the* L*ORD said, 'You had compassion on the plant, for which you did not work and which you did not cause to grow, which came up overnight and perished overnight. Should I not also have compassion on Nineveh, the great city in which there are more than 120,000 people?'" (Jonah 4:10-11)*

Here's the lesson: God loves and has compassion on all people everywhere who will turn to Him and worship and follow Him. He's made it plain to us in the gospel and through Jesus Christ, who died for all, that all might come to know Him. His love for us should create love in us for others. When it doesn't, something is wrong.

Here's the surprise: the book ends with a question instead of a conclusion. We know what Jonah *should* have said and what he *should* have done, but we're left without even a hint of how Jonah actually responded. It's as though God requires us to supply the answer for our own lives in the same way that Jonah was required to answer God in his.

God has a way of tearing at our outer shell, peeling back the layers, and exposing our hearts before saying, *Here is the problem*. As it did outside Nineveh, this usually happens when we're all alone, when personal comforts are removed and those rough spots never surrendered to God rise to the surface. Have you ever been there?

God may be saying to you, as He often says to me, *I want all of your heart. I deserve complete surrender from you.* This is almost always the issue—total surrender. Surrender is the clearest possible response when we trust God with our lives. It's that *faith* that is the character quality that shines through when I say yes instead of no to God.

There's a lot of Jonah in me. There's a lot of Jonah in most of us. What about you? Your story may not be as stark or as sensational, but you're still wondering if you've been put on the shelf for something done, or not done, in your past. It may be late, but it's never too late!

The greatest news is that we each have the chance to supply our own ending to the story of how much of ourselves and our heart we are willing to give to God.

You, and only you, can begin the journey of coming back from disobedience.

It begins with a yes instead of a no to what God is saying.

Chapter 5

After Darkness, Light

ELIJAH'S STORY

"Enough! Now, Lord, take my life."

1 Kings 19:4

Seven years into marriage, my wife and I experienced a dark night of the soul that we've come to call discouragement and depression. Neither of us knew what to do. We didn't even know what to call it. We were in our late 20s, with two children and another on the way. I would often come home from work to find Kim sitting on the stairs in tears and unable to tell me why.

She felt isolated and worthless, and had a sense of personal failure. She was battling impulses to run away and, more frighteningly, intense thoughts of suicide. We had no friends with this kind of experience that we were aware of, we knew no counselors at the time, and my theological training had left me unprepared. We had nowhere to turn.

Staring at each other, we wondered what the future held—or if there was a future. We honestly had no idea of what to do, and everything seemed so dark. Optimism was hard to find.

Unknowingly, we'd entered into a new season of life. It was a season we were not prepared for—and certainly a season for which we had no real game plan.

For years, depression was a dark, hidden, and solitary kind of hell for those who suffered from it. But today people are actually talking about discouragement and depression, and we often hear their stories.

Truthfully, we *must* talk about it because depression takes many forms and touches millions of lives. It now affects more than 264 million people worldwide, earning it the title of "leading cause of disability in the world" (World Health Organization, 2020, Singlecare.com).

Nearly all who are touched by depression experience seasons of persistent low moods. For many, an overwhelming sense of sadness and despair renders them unable to function in a healthy way—or at all. For some, suicide becomes an idea that seems to provide an escape from the dark clouds of depression.

The Way Out of Darkness

At the beginning of this chapter, I made a statement that was, for us, very real at the time: **we had nowhere to turn.** In those moments, it felt undeniable. We had no human help. No counselors, no helpful books, no friends we could share with and no support for what was happening. There was no "light." As I was a first-time pastor, there was also the expectation that our family should "have it all together." I now know that everyone feels that way.

When we eventually turned to God in desperation and began to search more deeply for answers that only by faith we felt must be there, we learned that He had given an incredible practical case study in Scripture for us to follow.

This brings me to a man named Elijah. Elijah's battle with disappointment and depression, leading to his desire to die, is amazingly relevant. You don't have to have a troubling background to get to a dark night of the soul. Elijah's background was stellar. He was a great prophet of God in the Old Testament time period, when there was no greater spiritual calling. He spoke for God, and to do that, you first had to hear from God. It was kind of a big deal. The most repeated phrase used to describe what Elijah said when he spoke for God is the phrase "by the word of the LORD." Elijah was not simply a bold prophet though. He also had a compassionate side to him. It was Elijah who, by the power of God, raised a boy from the dead and had mercy on a starving widow.

Elijah's crowning moment, however, came when he courageously and boldly confronted false prophets at Mount Carmel. He's famous for being a key player in the outrageous and eye-opening intervention in which God sent fire down from heaven to consume water-soaked wood placed on an altar. The confrontation, the prayer, and the resulting fire, followed by the astounding single-handed slaughter of 850 false prophets, raised the eyebrows and turned the hearts of an entire nation. The resulting revival of Israel positioned Elijah as a great leader—maybe one of the greatest in Israel's storied history. At the very least, Elijah seemed to have it all together with God, and was held in highest esteem in Israel.

But when the mountaintop experience of 1 Kings 18 moves into the valley experience of 1 Kings 19, we see how quickly things can change. We're reminded in the book of James that "Elijah was a man with a nature like ours." (James 5:17) This giant prophet of God was a man just like us. While James is telling us that we can pray like Elijah, it's also important to note that we can experience hardship like him, as well.

A Gauntlet of Discouragement and Depression

Have you ever experienced a gauntlet? To "run the gauntlet" is a form of punishment or trial where one is forced to run between two rows of people who strike out and attack as he runs through. To "throw down the gauntlet" means to challenge or confront someone. It always refers to severe trials. Trials in life sometimes are single, but often we experience waves of trials—at times, all at once.

In 1 Kings 19, Elijah is running the gauntlet, where he is attacked and wounded from every side. Read the account of Elijah's gauntlet, and you'll see all the elements we have to deal with as well.

> *"Now Ahab told Jezebel everything that Elijah had done, and how he had killed all the prophets with the sword. Then Jezebel sent a messenger to Elijah, saying, 'So may the gods do to me and more so, if by about this time tomorrow I do not make your life like the life of one of them.' And he was afraid, and got up and ran for his life and came to Beersheba, which belongs to Judah; and he left his servant there. But he himself went a day's journey into the wilderness, and came and sat down under a broom tree; and he asked for himself to die, and said, 'Enough! Now, LORD, take my life, for I am no better than my fathers.'" (1 Kings 19:1-4)*

Elijah's gauntlet had several sides to it. Yours may have more, but we can all identify with what Elijah was experiencing.

First, there was a sense of **emptiness**. This is one way to describe the effect of Elijah's physical and spiritual marathon of the previous few days. He'd had this huge confrontation on the mountaintop. On the backside of that mountaintop experience—just hours later—was a valley filled with difficult emotions. Can you imagine the spiritual intensity, the anxious waiting in prayer, and then the unbelievable physical exertion employed against hundreds of false prophets? And even though God came through in a powerful and unforgettable way, the next few hours were mundane and uneventful—compared to the mountain. God is not always seen and felt in ordinary days as He is on extraordinary ones. We love the fire on the mountaintop. We detest the silence of the valley.

Elijah also felt **opposition**. You'd think this victory would have been enough to remove the opposition, but it only stirred up Jezebel further. This was a truly wicked woman, and she was promising to take Elijah's life within 24 hours. There's a reason why we don't name our daughters "Jezebel." She was not only an angry woman; she was in a position of power and had the resources of the northern kingdom of Israel at her disposal. This was a real threat. But beyond that, this was spiritual opposition. Elijah had done what God had told him to do, and it's almost impossible to understand why that was not "enough."

There was also **fearfulness**. He was afraid because of Jezebel's threats and seems to have forgotten God's power previously on the mountain. It's so easy to forget that the God who is mighty on the mountain is also mighty in the valley. I've noticed that fear often gets the best of people—it is such a common experience in life. Sometimes that fear leads us to make the wrong decisions, choosing to isolate from those who can help and encourage us, and we sometimes come to believe that those fears are more real than they are. Paul told Timothy:

> *"For God has not given us a spirit of fear, but of power and of love and of a sound mind."*
>
> *(2 Timothy 1:7, NKJV)*

To make things even worse, Elijah experiences **loneliness**. He has made the mistake of leaving his trusted servant and moving into the wilderness alone. All he's got left is the echo chamber of a mind that has turned dark. He's forgotten his need for interaction, for reminders of God's faithfulness, and for someone to correct his crooked thinking. If you struggle with depression, don't create loneliness for yourself. It never helps to be all alone in this dark time.

If you know someone who struggles, their silence is a yellow flag at the very least, and possibly a red flag. Silence is a reminder that we need other people to help us through. Stay connected—which is the opposite of what Elijah did.

As if these are not enough, he also battles **weariness**. Leaving his servant behind, he's gone yet another day into the wilderness alone. What's driving him is the hope that he can outrun his enemy—and in running he's spiraling into further weariness and weakness. What he needs is rest. What he gets is exhaustion.

Finally, he feels **there is no future**. He's deciding that God is done with him. He doesn't have any answers, even though he knows well who can help him. You don't arrive at "Take my life" without sinking into a very, very dark cloud. Elijah was saying, *I give up, God. I don't know what else I can do.*

C.S. Lewis was on point when he said:

> *"Mental pain is less dramatic than physical pain, but is more common and also harder to bear. The frequent attempt to conceal mental pain increases the burden; it is easier to say, 'My tooth is aching' than to say, 'My heart is broken.'" (The Problem of Pain)*

I've never tortured myself physically, but I certainly have lashed myself mentally, causing deeper and longer-lasting scars. I suspect most of us have. If you have, you know the relentless gauntlet of self-condemnation. No wonder the enemy of our soul uses it so well. Beyond that, it is this mental torture—this wrestling with all the wrong perceived facts and realities that spirals us downward into depression.

Do I Really Know How This Ends?

The situation is rarely as awful as it feels. Further, our story almost never ends up the way we fear it will—that is, unless we conclude the story ourselves. At some point in our battle against depression, we have to confess, "God, I am empty, fearful, and lonely. I've lost hope." It's good to come to an end *of ourselves*.

Elijah was at this place—and he was as open and vulnerable with God as a person can be. It's more than notable—it's actually a huge spotlight on the conversation—that Elijah said these words to God and not merely to himself.

Note his prayer closely. It's vastly different to say, "Enough! Now, LORD, take my life" rather than *It is enough; now I will take my life*. Do you see the difference? One statement speaks to God; the other speaks to self. One leaves the conclusion to God; the other takes it into our own hands.

We cannot conclude what is not ours to conclude. We cannot end what is not ours to end. We're not wired to make a decision of that magnitude, and we're not capable of foreseeing what the future holds. Ultimately, we must acknowledge God as the Lord of life and death. Who are we to end our life, which God has created? Who are we to declare that things cannot change for the better and that God doesn't have something ahead for us in this life?

Elijah acknowledges this in his desperate cry to God. Even though things seem completely out of control to him, he still believes God has the final say. And because he has cried out and continues on, his life takes a dramatic and unpredictable turn for the better.

A Messenger of Hope

Years ago, I heard this old story. There was a man whose house and land were completely flooded. He was alone on the roof, trusting God to save him. A boat came by, but he refused to go with the rescuers, saying he was trusting God. A helicopter came by as well, but he turned down the offer of rescue, because he was going to just trust God. Finally, the water covered him completely, and he drowned. Later he stood before God. He wondered why God had not helped him in the flood. God replied, "Did you not see the boat and the helicopter I sent you?"

This story, while somewhat corny, makes a good point and illustrates a principle to believe in. God is always aware and always able to send help to us. We sometimes don't recognize it is Him, but He sends help, nonetheless.

In 1 Kings 19, God sends an angel for Elijah to be encouraged by. What happens next is significant for all of us.

> *"The angel of the LORD came again a second time and touched him and said, 'Arise, eat, because the journey is too great for you.' So he arose and ate and drank, and went in the strength of that food forty days and forty nights to Horeb, the mountain of God."*
>
> *(1 Kings 19:7-8, NASB95)*

The presence of this angel is simple but profound. God has sent someone to Elijah.

God sends an angel because Elijah *needs* an angel. This is an intervention in Elijah's life to get him from dark to light. Sometimes we need an angel to intervene for us, and sometimes we need to be an angel ourselves in intervening for others. I can count several times when God sent or led another person to speak an important, timely word to me at a dark time. This is why we are not helping ourselves when we cut off other people during times of darkness.

In Scripture, whether Old or New Testament, angels are messengers to bring a message from God. And the message here is, *Elijah, you have somewhere else to be. It's time to get going.* This is how God works. Whether by angel or by another human, God is speaking to Elijah.

I don't want to oversimplify this moment. This *is* a supernatural event. Elijah's visitor *is* an angel. Elijah *is* found in a remote place. Then he *does* run forty days on the food the angel has given him. God was unwilling to leave him alone, weak, and hopeless. Even if no other person comes to Elijah—because no other person was present—this angel comes as a messenger from God.

The prophet had already been resting. He'd slept under a broom (or juniper) tree and was sleeping when the angel came. Elijah needed to be with someone, so the angel came and touched him. A touch from another person, or even from an angel, is powerful. Elijah also needed to get up and eat. There are things you can do on your feet that you'll never be able to do on a bed.

A mentor of mine has a helpful piece of counsel. He says that we are most vulnerable to sin, selfishness, and Satan when we are...

Hungry
Anxious
Lonely
Tired

I've found this to be true over the years. When I realize that I'm experiencing an unusual amount of one or more of these four elements in my life, I need to "HALT" and replenish. Looking back, my wife Kim would say that she was lonely and tired much of the time when she struggled with depression.

We need to seek rest. We need refreshment. We also need to find community—people around us who care. That's why the church can and should be our people when we're in need. This is why God calls people to the ministry of encouragement and counseling. It's also why God gives us the ability to pray—and assures us He hears us.

Psalm 22 records the heartfelt cry of "Why have You forsaken me?" (v 1). It is followed by "In You our fathers trusted; They trusted and You delivered them ... and [they] were not disappointed" (v 4-5).

Reach out to God. Remember how He has come through for others.

A Meeting with God

Many significant encounters in the Bible have three key parts. One is the personal element—the person's dilemma. Then, there is a human element that includes what others around the person are doing and saying. Finally, there is a climactic moment when God meets with them and their life is changed. With Elijah, it involved God demonstrating His power over nature before whispering to him in a still, quiet voice. He knows how to get our attention.

> *"And behold, a voice came to him and said, 'What are you doing here, Elijah?' Then he said, 'I have been very zealous for the LORD, the God of hosts; for the sons of Israel have forsaken Your covenant, torn down Your altars and killed Your prophets with the sword. And I*

> *alone am left; and they seek my life, to take it away.' The* LORD *said to him, 'Go, return on your way to the wilderness of Damascus.'"* (1 Kings 19:13-15, NASB95)

As my wife, Kim, worked through her discouragement and depression, her questions were: *Will anything ever change in life? God, do you understand how I'm feeling? What do I do when I don't know what to do?*

We don't always have all the answers that we want. But God does. And He still allows people to encounter Him while they are in the darkness.

My experience of 35 years of pastoring churches, counseling, and my personal times of needing to have an encounter with God myself, leads me to encourage you as loudly and clearly as I possibly can: *God is still there. God still cares, and God still speaks to people today.*

I can't tell you exactly how God will reveal Himself in your specific situation. I'm not suggesting that you go stand on a mountain somewhere and expect God to audibly speak to you, though I wouldn't put that past Him. He can do that, and He has. Here's what I can do. I can tell you ways in which He often has met with people like you and me, and I can help you look for those in your own situation. Look at how God met with Elijah.

God asks questions. "What are you doing here, Elijah?" God is not asking in order to get information. In His omniscience, He knows everything from eternity past to eternity future. He's the God who declares the end from the beginning. God doesn't need information. God asks questions to help *us* become aware of what's happening.

In the Garden of Eden, He asked Adam, "Where are you?" (Genesis 3:9).

In the book of Job, God asks righteous Job, who was suffering badly and wondering how God balances good and evil, "Where were you when I laid the foundation of the earth?" (Job 38:4).

Again, God asks questions to help *us* become aware of what's happening to us and to help us realize where our actions are taking us. God asks questions because the truth about where we are usually hasn't fully dawned on us yet. We're aware something is not right, but we're not sure why.

Hence the question to Elijah, "What are you doing here?" *Why are you in the wilderness? Why are you running? Why have you wearied yourself and abandoned your post? What do you think you will accomplish with all these things?*

More than a few times, the Lord has asked me questions. *Why are you thinking this way? What did I tell you to do? Why do you hesitate?*

God adjusts perspectives. Elijah's answer to God reveals his limited perspective. Up to this point, all Elijah has talked about is himself and the threat to his life at the hands of Jezebel. He's consumed with fear and disappointment. He describes his zeal for God and speaks as though there is no one else on earth who is willing to serve God. He cannot fathom how God will allow the one person who is serving Him to die.

Long ago, this story led me to a truth that has served many well: self-pity and self-piety are enemies of a balanced perspective. If I believe that no one else is suffering like I am, and if I believe that I am undeserving of this hardship, I cannot possibly see the whole picture, and find myself consumed by the little I do see.

With this gentle encounter, God tells Elijah what is next, and it has nothing to do with Elijah's death—but with his future. God speaks truth to Elijah's speculation. Elijah thinks he alone serves God, but God says there are 7,000 others who have not bowed the knee to Baal. This radically changes Elijah's perspective.

God gives direction. Once God has our attention, He usually gives direction. Elijah thinks it's time for him to die, but God tells him that there is more for him to do and places a specific plan before him. We all need next steps.

In the end, God gives purpose. In Elijah's case, surprisingly, it was nothing new. It was the purpose he had always had as a prophet but had lost through his suffering and fear. God simply affirmed to Elijah that *This is still what I want you to do.* It was enough to get Elijah up and moving forward again.

When we need Him the most, God is able to ask questions, adjust perspectives, and give direction. In fact, this is exactly what we ought to pray for when we're in the valley. *What am I unaware of that I need to know? How am I not believing You in this circumstance? What are You asking me to do?*

When you're in the darkness, and when you don't know what you need to do, pray this way. Then wait for the answers you need to move ahead. You will find them.

After the Darkness of Night, Light Breaks Through

Kim and I experienced a comeback from depression in the months following what was described in the opening pages of this chapter. Within months, life began to make more sense, and joy began to be experienced again. Now, after decades of marriage and the challenge of raising of six children, I see that beautiful smile often. We're both very grateful.

And what about Elijah? Well, the story gets better. Elijah goes on and does what God asks of him, and eventually anoints a successor—the prophet Elisha.

Remember the person he feared the most and the reason why he ran into the wilderness? It was the threat of death at the hands of wicked Jezebel within 24 hours. It never happened. God used Elijah to prophesy Jezebel's death and the gruesome manner in which it would occur. Further, God used Jehu, whom Elijah anointed, to bring it about. In other words, Elijah's obedience in anointing a successor was the answer to his fears.

By the way, if you're familiar with this story, do you recall exactly how Elijah's life in this world ended? In 2 Kings 2, we read the following:

> *"As they were going along and talking, behold, there appeared a chariot of fire and horses of fire which separated the two of them. And Elijah went up by a whirlwind to heaven." (2 Kings 2:11, NASB95)*

There's no record of Elijah's death in the Bible. It's conspicuously absent. Many biblical scholars would say that he didn't die, and that God will be using him in the end times. So, all that he was afraid of never came to pass.

We know so little of the big picture. What we do know is that we can entrust it to God. As we do, we can be sure to encounter a God who is big enough to restore our lives.

Chapter 6

Difficult People and the Goodness of God

ABIGAIL'S STORY

"Now then, be aware and consider what you should do."

1 Samuel 25:17

The disturbing thing about writing this chapter is not the absence of modern-day examples of people in our own culture who face mistreatment or oppression but the *abundance* of them.

I've become familiar over the years with several couples in fractured marriages. In most cases, the woman was suffering, and weighty decisions that had to be made were placed on her. As this happened, she would have to walk through one of the most difficult seasons of her life.

Having to navigate between pacifying an angry, inconsiderate spouse and providing nurture, protection, and provision for her family is an unbelievable task. Add to that the loneliness of keeping it all together and you have a picture of real hardship.

I love that the Bible doesn't avoid addressing messed-up situations like this. I'm grateful that there are examples of people who've lived through this kind of hard season and who found that God does indeed see and care and give grace.

A woman named Abigail was one of them.

I'm not sure how I've managed to merely skim the details of the story of Abigail through the years, but I have recently discovered great treasure in the account of her life. In a single chapter of the Bible, her life comes and goes, but it stands as a lighthouse of wisdom and hope for those who face extraordinary difficulty and oppression in relationships.

This is not a story about marriage, though she's in a difficult marriage. This story is about being ready in the moment for unpredictable and critical decisions—it's about how we handle people in our lives who are angry and hell-bent on destruction. It's about margins and trust—and in the end, making the kinds of statements and taking the kinds of actions that help us navigate dangerous moments.

Reading the first three verses of 1 Samuel 25, you get the Instagram photo version of Abigail's life. She is married to a man named Nabal, who is "very rich" and who has 3,000 sheep and 1,000 goats (v 2). This is a massive ranch with thousands of acres, isolated from population centers. Abigail is "intelligent and beautiful in appearance" (v 3). A beautiful woman with a massive ranch and an inheritance to oversee.

It sounds idyllic right up until the last line of verse 3: "but the man was harsh and evil in his dealings."

The Greatest Challenges in Life

Some of our greatest challenges in life have nothing to do with physical circumstances, catastrophes, or temptations. They have to do with people.

Harsh and evil people. Toxic people. Angry people. Messed-up people who put us in harm's way by their actions and attitudes. Oppressive people. Even abusive ones. All of that is found here, in Abigail's marriage.

Of course, not all the difficult people we encounter are in marriages. At times we will encounter dilemmas inflicted by people who produce in us a paralyzing fear that we have to work through. We need an example of how someone walks through heightened tensions and moments of panic to see that good things still happen in the end. This chapter will call our attention to dealing with angry friends, coworkers, and neighbors and many tough life situations.

The story of Abigail travels through some cliff-hanging moments when you wonder what will happen. But God brings her through it all—and takes her to a place that no one could predict.

Abigail's story reveals how God uses our circumstances and the difficult people around us in redemptive ways. If He did this with Abigail, He can do it with you.

Abigail is the wife of this wealthy landowner in the wilderness at a time when a young king-to-be named David is roaming the wilderness of Paran with hundreds of loyal warriors. David is a fearless leader. He didn't back down from a giant named Goliath, so he isn't afraid of anyone else either. He's used to getting his way.

On the other side of this story is harsh, evil Nabal, who owns the land on which David and his band have been roaming (see 1 Samuel 25:15-16). Nabal is preparing for a banquet day, and David's hungry soldiers know food is being readied—food that they have helped protect by their presence. The smell of a meal is in the air, so David sends ten of his men to request a favor of Nabal.

> *"Therefore let my young men find favor in your eyes, for we have come on a festive day. Please give whatever you*

> *find at hand to your servants and to your son David."*
> *(1 Samuel 25:8)*

The response from Nabal is true to his character—harsh and evil.

> *"Who is David? And who is the son of Jesse? ... Shall I then take my bread and my water and my meat that I have slaughtered for my shearers, and give it to men whose origin I do not know?" (v 10-11)*

It's a moment of obvious disrespect. Everyone knew who David was. Every person in Israel knew of his battle skills, his courage, and his anointing as the next king. But Nabal didn't acknowledge any of that, and now we have two angry men, ready to face off and shed blood. David commands 400 men to strap on their swords, and they head to Nabal's house, with David personally leading the way.

There is no hopeful way to see this. Blood will be shed. Someone will have to back down, and neither of these men seem to have it in them to do that. It's a death sentence for Nabal and his entire family if things are allowed to progress. There is no other logical outcome. There is no law enforcement in this wilderness. There is no one to call on for help.

A Defining Moment in Life

Nothing and no one stands between David and Nabal's house. No one, that is, except one woman: Abigail.

In the first three verses of 1 Samuel 25, I can think of a few people who'd want to be in her shoes. In the next 17 verses, not so many. No one wants to be in such a lose-lose situation.

Her husband is not going to back down, nor is this young king-in-waiting. Neither man seems to have enough sense at this moment to engage in dialogue or negotiation. This leaves Abigail, her household, and David's warriors at the mercy of what these two men decide.

It's hard to imagine how God can use something so toxic as this scenario, but God wants you to see that unfair, oppressive activities are not outside His redemptive ability to change. At the very least, it should bring us hope. It might even help give us the wisdom that Abigail displayed.

Abigail's story also shows us **the kind of character that God honors.** This entire story begins to shift in a single moment when Abigail is told what is going to happen. The young man who brings her the news says it plainly:

> *"Now then, be aware and consider what you should do, because harm is plotted against our master and against all his household; and he is such a worthless man that no one can speak to him."* (v 17)

David and his men are bearing down on Nabal's house and on all that he owns. Nabal is too angry and out of control to be spoken to. The young man makes it clear: Abigail is the only person who can rescue this household.

It is at this moment that her character kicks in, and she is admirable in every way.

She Takes Responsibility

You might think, "Wait a moment. She's beautiful. She's wealthy. She's not part of this battle. Surely she could save herself when David comes riding in." But what would happen to Nabal? What would happen to all her faithful servants? What about the rest of her family?

Others will point out what a great opportunity this would be to get rid of wicked Nabal and presumably a bad marriage, but Abigail doesn't see it that way. Abigail sees herself as part of the entire household and knows that if she doesn't defend them, they'll all perish.

It rests on her to do something to change the situation. There are times in life when fairness is not part of the picture. It's not fair that Nabal or David places her in this situation. It's not fair that the servants are too weak to protect her in this moment. But there's no time for her to question matters of fairness.

Abigail steps up. She hurries. She surveys the resources available to her, takes a deep breath, no doubt mumbles a prayer of quiet desperation, and walks into the fire these men have set.

She meets David at the bottom of the mountain which he is descending. While he's breathing threats about killing every man in Nabal's house, she's considering what her words will be. With her is the food, wine, and sheep that Nabal should have offered David. She's taken the best of the feast that's been prepared.

And she hasn't told Nabal. Perhaps Abigail's entire life has been spent earning trust and walking with Nabal in whatever way was needed. And on this occasion, she steps out alone because she has no real choice. Perhaps it is the exception, not the rule, but it saves his life.

She is intervening for her household. She is owning the situation as best she can. She is standing in the gap for all those who will not and cannot. In this situation, and in most others, someone must say, "I'll take responsibility." That is just good leadership, and a great practical principle for us all.

Why does this not surprise us? It's not surprising because we know women just like this who have had to own situations that were not created by them, and who rescue people close to them. Abigail is showing the kind of responsibility that multitudes of moms I know would display.

She Shows Respect

Her servant has explained what's happened between David's men and Nabal. She knows that the anointed one and his warriors have been disrespected, so with the food she brings the appropriate respect that was never given. This isn't about hunger anymore. It's a moment when basic dignity and respect need to be shown. What happens in this conversation changes the future.

> *"When Abigail saw David, she hurried and dismounted from her donkey, and fell on her face in front of David and bowed herself to the ground." (1 Samuel 25:23)*

In her appeal to David, Abigail uses the term "my lord" 14 times. In 24 different ways we see respect being shown in these verses.

One lesson we learn here is that it is much better to approach people—including those who are being ungodly—with respect rather than with demands. Abigail knew this and utilized that knowledge in approaching David.

She Exercises Restraint

Abigail does something here that is extraordinary. She shows the restraint and wisdom to David that she hopes he himself will have. In other words, she leads the way for this future king to act wisely to preserve his future. She tells David that she believes God will give him great victories and place him properly on the throne of Israel. *However*, she says, *you do not want an incident of bloodshed here today to haunt you.*

> *"This will not become an obstacle to you, or a troubled heart to my lord, both by having shed blood without cause and by my lord's having avenged himself." (v 31)*

This is a stunning moment, when a woman in the wilderness is modeling for a future king the power and security of restraint. While we have no way of knowing whether Abigail realizes this as it unfolds, we can see that God has placed her here to rescue a king.

Think about your future, she says. And he does. David sees that she is making more sense than he is—and realizes that he needs to listen to this woman.

Men everywhere should note this moment. If one of the greatest kings in history listened to a woman who had more wisdom than him, shouldn't we? Many times, as I charge forward in some direction I have in mind, my wife will speak up with a voice of reason.

But the biggest thing Abigail does in this conversation is something we should all do.

She remembers the Lord.

This has a profound effect on the conversation.

David rides in talking about himself—who he is and what he'll do. David is lamenting the disrespect given to him. David is talking about revenge and vindication. David has lost sight of the Lord.

Oswald Chambers famously said, "Once we lose sight of God, we become reckless." It's an incredibly true observation echoed throughout Scripture, and especially here in this passage. We might even admit our own familiarity with this principle. How often have we forgotten and lost sight of God?

On the other hand, Abigail is talking about the Lord.

> *"As the LORD lives ... the LORD has restrained you ... for the LORD will certainly make for my lord an enduring house, because my lord is fighting the battles of the LORD, and evil will not be found in you." (v 26-28)*

Abigail was beautiful, she was intelligent, and likely her

argument was persuasive, but it was when she spoke about the Lord that David was brought back to reality. Suddenly, David realized *This is about God and me, not Nabal and me.* What a game changer! Interestingly, as soon as Abigail starts talking about God, David brings the Lord into the conversation, as well.

> *"Blessed be the LORD God of Israel, who sent you this day to meet me, and blessed be your discernment, and blessed be you, who have kept me this day from bloodshed." (v 32-33)*

David has backed down. He has seen what is happening. The fact that David responds well tells us a great deal about his own character. Immediately, he speaks wisdom:

> *"Go up to your house in peace. See I have listened to you and granted your request." (v 35)*

When Character Is Everything

Abigail's character has brought her through. It's true that character is *forged* in the fire, but it's even more obvious that character is *revealed* in the fire. Hers is here for us to see.

Your character is what will get you through the storm. Stay true to *who* you are, no matter *where* you are. And *who* you are is this: a greatly loved child of God, saved by the death of His Son, and indwelled by His Spirit. Scripture is full of examples of those whose characters are based on faith in Him and are being transformed by Him. Joseph's character got him through prison. Daniel's character brought him through the lions' den. It is Abigail's character that shines through in this story.

As God develops your character in difficult situations, learn to lean on the right kinds of responses and the right kinds of mindsets that the Lord teaches us to have. These will guard your heart and mind, as they did with Abigail.

Her character is there regardless of how this story turns out. So is yours. No matter how people might react when you demonstrate character and speak about the Lord, it's still the right thing to do.

But there's more.

Abigail and her family are safe for the moment, but she still hasn't told Nabal. The toxic man in the background of this story is still in the picture, feasting away at the banquet he's prepared and by now completely drunk. I can only imagine the dread she faced in giving him the news of her intervention with David on his behalf.

Abigail summoned the courage the next morning to tell him what she'd done, and Nabal's response was so catastrophic that he collapsed and never moved again. The Bible says, "About ten days later, the LORD struck Nabal and he died" (v 38).

Suddenly, the noise and commotion of such a huge confrontation is silenced. I can see Abigail sitting down in the quiet, wondering how the intensity of the previous few days had so permanently gone away—and contemplating what would be next for her.

God doesn't always solve our dilemma by someone's death. Sometimes, we *outlive* the threats in our lives. I can say that about many adversarial situations in my life.

As we get to the remaining verses describing her life, we see how God takes difficult circumstances and redeems them beyond imagination. Obviously, He honors Abigail's character in getting her through the impossible situations she's encountered.

But God isn't through. There are powerful, inspiring practical principles for us here.

It's Never Too Late

It's never too late for peace. David's instruction to Abigail, "Go up to your house in peace," concluded a war in the making and placed her household out of harm's way. If we were to break this day of confrontation into time segments, I'd conclude that it is *deep* into this situation before God shows up and changes things. God waits to the end. He's a 4th-quarter kind of God.

Have you ever heard this phrase? "God is rarely early, but He's never late." I heard it for many years before I realized just how true it was in nearly every desperate circumstance and situation. I'm never sure about God's timing, but the way He works (rarely early and all) often leaves me in a place of desperate trust. I suspect that's true of you as well. Remember the exodus of Israel? Before intervening God waited until the Egyptians, with their 600 plus chariots, drew near to the retreating Israelites, who had stopped at the Red Sea (Exodus 14). He's a *rarely early, never late* kind of God.

Remember Jesus' rescue of Lazarus? Coming to Lazarus' tomb *four days after he had died*, Jesus is met by Martha, who says, "Lord, if You had been here, my brother would not have died" (John 11:21). Of course, to us this seems late, but Jesus nonetheless performed the miracle of raising Lazarus back to life. He's never late—often He turns everything around in this life, and always He does so at the end of this life, when on the day we die He brings us through death and out the other side to life with Him.

God is also never done with you, no matter how far behind the curve you feel. I've known people who have lost so much, and yet, when God changes them and their circumstance, all that was lost is regained. Remember Job?

It's never too late for love. Nabal died, and when David heard about it, his first thought was to bless the Lord for restraining him from killing Nabal in a rage. He knew he'd been rescued from gaining a horrific reputation that could have threatened his ability to lead Israel.

His second thought was Abigail. David could not forget the beautiful woman who had rescued him that day—and who had helped preserve his future kingdom.

I have a habit of saying over and over as I read the pages of Scripture, "Somebody needs to make a movie out of this!" The story of Abigail and David is such a phenomenal love story. While it's true she was beautiful, I doubt it was her beauty that captured his heart. David, I surmise, was most captured by her character and her wisdom, and considered her indispensable to him.

David's son, Solomon, echoed this kind of truth many years later when he wrote, "Charm is deceitful and beauty is vain, but a woman who fears the Lord, she shall be praised" (Proverbs 31:30).

It's never too late for new beginnings. Not only could David not forget Abigail, but he knew he needed her to be his queen. Whether it was David's desire to have her for himself, or the Lord's provision for the future kingdom of Israel, or both, it serves to remind us of new beginnings.

> *"Then David sent a proposal to Abigail, to take her as his wife." (1 Samuel 25:39)*

She wasted no time, quickly saddling a donkey, and with five women servants, she made her way to become a wife of David and a future queen of Israel. There is so much in this moment that is left to our imagination. At the very least, Abigail realized a peace, a love and a new beginning beyond anything she could have expected.

When we are in times of desperation and misery, is it

too much to think that God may have bigger plans and a greater future than we dare to hope? His plans for Abigail were certainly bigger than she could imagine.

As I think about the testimony of so many who've faced similar situations, I'm encouraged by the character I've seen in their lives and the new season they eventually experienced. God has been faithful to them, as He was to Abigail.

We don't know much more about this amazing woman named Abigail. We know she became David's wife and bore a child after David became king in Hebron, whom she named Chileab, which means "restraint."

We never hear of her again. Her moment of fame and influence was brief and powerful. She changed her world by being the right woman in the right place at the right time. She left a lasting example of character and trust.

Her story also stands as an encouragement for so many who go through the same kind of fire and call out to the God who rescued Abigail.

Chapter 7

After You've Blown It

DAVID'S STORY

"My sin is constantly before me."

Psalm 51:3

People can come back from moral failure—even when it seems impossible.

The woman I visited with in my office one day had a fascinating story. Amber (not her real name) and her husband were members of our church, and they were both in leadership classes I taught. Serious about their faith and the study of Scripture, both exhibited a vibrant and growing walk with God.

Over the course of our conversation, she referred to a past time in her life when she was without Christ, and said, "I was a sex worker, you know."

I hope no surprise registered on my face, but I *was* surprised by her statement. As a pastor, I'm privileged to hear many amazing "before and after" stories where there is literally no other explanation in the change of life apart from God—but Amber's story reminded me once again of how powerful God is.

Amber would go on to tell of several bad seasons in

life—"dark seasons" she calls them—when she tried to fill the void in her heart. Finally, she said to God, "I give up. I can't do this anymore." She placed her faith in Jesus and began to trust Him to save her and change her life. It was obvious to me that He had done just that.

While Amber is quick to say that her transformation was not easy and did not happen overnight, she also is a living testimony of God's cleansing, saving, transforming power. He really can and *does* bring people back from dark seasons of sin and disobedience.

Scripture teaches us about the very direct results of sin when it tells us that sin separates us from fellowship with God. That broken fellowship is the result of any sin, not just moral sin like David's. Though not simply a book of rules, the Bible teaches us that living life by our desires, by our own stubborn ways, and by our own selfish ambition will always keep us from intimacy with Jesus.

In this way, all sin is alike. Some of us may suffer greater consequences from certain acts of disobedience, but it all separates us from the best life God has for us. I can vividly recall moments when God explicitly warned me about a sinful habit that needed to be dealt with if I were to walk closely with Him—and I knew He was serious!

The book of Proverbs states it plainly when it comes to the consequences of sin and what we do with it: "One who conceals his wrongdoings will not prosper, but one who confesses and abandons them will find compassion" (Proverbs 28:13).

The Truth about Sin

King David knew this truth by experience, and it shows up in his story.

King David had committed the most infamous act of adultery in the history of the world.

It's not exactly the kind of fame anyone should desire, but David's liaison with Bathsheba, while at the height of his leadership and power, was recorded in the Scriptures and is as well-known as any sin in history.

When you come to know the man named in David in the Bible, you meet a man of many contrasts. He's a surprising character who comes seemingly out of nowhere.

David is chosen by God and anointed to be the future king by Samuel while he is a 15-year-old shepherd boy, herding sheep on a hillside, the youngest son of the house of Jesse and the least likely to become king. He becomes a surprising hero of the nation of Israel when he slays the giant, Goliath, to rescue his people from certain embarrassment and defeat. He then spends years running from King Saul, who is jealous of David's popularity and anointing. Saul finally dies, and David becomes king.

David is both powerful and humble. Anointed and unassuming. Wise and foolish.

His role as a king and his gift as a psalmist mean that we have more intimate glimpses into his life than any with other Old Testament character. We read amazing details about his life, his rule, and his sin.

The Bible positions David as a man after God's own heart, and often in his early days he was an exemplary leader. King David did, however, enter into a season of secret sin and humiliation. The familiar story can be summarized in just a few words.

It doesn't take long to fall.

David's humiliation transpired when he took the wife a soldier in the Israelite army who was at war, bedded her while her husband was on the front lines, impregnated her, and attempted to cover it up by arranging the death of her husband, Uriah. David then had his sin exposed by the prophet Nathan, whom God sent to call him out.

To read Nathan's exposure of David's sin is painful. God used this prophet like a surgeon's scalpel, getting to the core of a cancerous tumor of sin in David's life.

> *"You yourself are the man!" (2 Samuel 12:7)*

> *"Indeed, you did it secretly, but I will do this thing before all Israel, and in open daylight." (v 12)*

Because of David's wicked choice, he is now in free fall, and no one can stop him.

Confession Changes Everything

No one can stop his fall—that is, except David himself; and he does it with confession.

> *"I have sinned against the LORD." (v 13)*

This is a moment of truth that halts his rebellious slide. It is the acknowledgment to God of what he's done. From this confession onward, David begins the walk back to the God who forgives.

> *"And Nathan said to David, 'The LORD has allowed your sin to pass; you shall not die.'" (v 13b)*

Sin is devastating, but this is the story we all need to hear—that of *coming back from sin* and recognizing that God is not through with us. Before we tell that story, three important observations must be made.

Sin is always a setback. This is not debatable. Somehow, sin will make you pay.

Sin is never in secret. Like David, we think we may get away with it. Sin will find us out.

Sin is not the end. We may feel like sin has ended us, but there is a way out.

Psalm 51 is David's prayer of response to the exposure of

his sin—and it is recorded for all posterity to see and learn from. It is what you have if you take a weeping, grieving, repentant heart, and put it into words. It is an amazingly powerful and vulnerable expression to God.

The prayer of Psalm 51 shows us much that we need to know about coming back from sin. It's marked well in my Bible because I've been here many times. Allow me to highlight some principles here...

1. When You Come Back to God, Do It Directly

> *"Be gracious to me, God, according to Your faithfulness; According to the greatness of Your compassion, wipe out my wrongdoings." (Psalm 51:1)*

David does not look to a priest or religion as the pathway back. He's not trying to self-atone or pay a penalty that will free him from sin's consequences.

He knows he has offended God, so he comes straight to God, the Judge *and* the Forgiver. He appeals to God's character: specifically to His loving-kindness and compassion.

Normally, our first response is to run *from* God. After all, that's what the first man and woman did in the Garden of Eden. They hid from God. They were exposed, naked, and ashamed. So they "hid" from the God who sees all and knows all. And still God approached them to deal with their sin.

Most of us know that we ultimately cannot run from God, and yet we sometimes try to. It's painful to be reminded of friends, coworkers or acquaintances who have given in to sexual sin while ignoring God, their loved ones, and others—and to watch their lives disintegrate. It's difficult to watch life disintegrate from sin or compromise, but it's tragically predictable. Sowing always brings reaping.

David doesn't run away from God in an attempt to hide, but he runs to God, throwing himself on the mercy of the God who forgives.

It's like the prodigal son but in the Old Testament.

Maybe you've heard of the parable of the prodigal son, the story Jesus told about a privileged son who demanded his inheritance in advance and spent it on riotous living (Luke 15:11-32). Far from his father and deep in misery and brokenness, he finally came to the end of himself and headed home—straight into the unexpected and waiting arms of his loving father.

Jesus throws us a curve ball with this parable. We *understand* the son's desire to go home. Who wouldn't want to go home if you were broke or broken? That's no surprise. We also *identify* with the son's statement: "Treat me as one of your hired laborers" (v 19). He deserves to pay for his foolishness, we think.

The surprise of Jesus' parable is the open, loving, forgiving, and restoring arms of the compassionate father. This is radical love. It seems unreasonable to us—but it's how God loves us. How do I know this? Because it's *Jesus* who tells this story, and no one knows the Father like Jesus does. If you've been away from God, this should be music to your soul.

This concept of God's character is not found just in a prayer or a parable. This truth is found throughout Scripture. The apostle Paul, writing to the church in Rome, says, "Or do you think lightly of the riches of His kindness and restraint and patience, not knowing that the kindness of God leads you to repentance?" (Romans 2:4).

This is the God to whom David, in Psalm 51, is running directly—as fast as he can. He's running into his Father's arms, begging for mercy and forgiveness. In running back to God, he's running away from his sin—which is what repentance is: a full turn.

This is the first step back. No matter how far away the Father seems, you must come to Him and appeal to His mercy, loving-kindness, and forgiveness. It's just a step, but it's a huge step in the right direction—and for David, it was a complete about-face to turn to the Father in prayer.

We can imagine what was going through the mind of David. Here is a king who had faced a warrior giant as a 15-year-old. He had chased away lions and bears who came after the sheep he was watching in his father's fields. He faced the armies of his enemies with boldness and abandon, and he knew victory after victory.

He was no coward, but there is something intimidating about facing God when you've failed Him, which makes us want to avoid it at all costs. And yet, we cannot turn away from God if we ever hope to come back from sin.

2. When You Come Back to God, Take Ownership for Sin

Sin is tantalizing, isn't it? It lies to us. It makes us think it will be all pleasure—all good. *No one will be hurt*, sin says. *No one will know*, temptation calls out. But afterwards, it's worse than we could have imagined. David says:

> *"For I know my wrongdoings, and my sin is constantly before me." (Psalm 51:3)*

It was a full year after his sin when Nathan confronted David, and the child of David and Bathsheba died. During those months, David's sin was *ever* before him. He could not get it out of his mind. Every glance at Bathsheba, every sidelong look from his palace officials, every mention of battle, and his sin came rushing back into focus. His life was now far from where it should have been.

In another of David's psalms, he described sin's effect on himself:

> *"For Your arrows have sunk deep into me, and Your hand has pressed down on me. There is no healthy part in my flesh because of Your indignation; There is no health in my bones because of my sin. For my guilty deeds have gone over my head; Like a heavy burden they weigh too much for me ... I feel faint and badly crushed; I groan because of the agitation of my heart." (Psalm 38:2-4, 8)*

If you're still in sin, you already know this feeling. If you're considering walking into sin, you should read this passage a few times and try it on for size. It describes your future in sin's grip. It's weighty, it's heavy, and it's burdensome—the effects of sin are spiritual, psychological, *and* physical.

If all this is foreign to you, remind yourself of the last time you were estranged from someone you really loved and didn't want to lose. Maybe you hurt them badly. Perhaps you offended them by what you said, or betrayed them, or broke their trust.

If you can imagine that moment, that sinking feeling in the pit of your stomach may actually return to you—even now. The anger and disgust of the one you offended might come rushing back to your mind as if it were yesterday. The memory of separation and the loneliness of having lost a friend may again haunt your thoughts.

Magnify that painful memory by a thousand times and imagine that it's God you've offended. That's where David was.

There's a point in all the pain sin brings. The point is that we take ownership.

We live in a world that blames others. Our tendency is to point to the nature of the tempter or the temptation. We cry "foul" when things seem unfair, and we respond in a wrong way. We're reluctant—even stubbornly resistant—to take the blame.

There is no healing in blaming others. There are no solutions. It deflects. It allows us to dodge responsibility.

In Jesus' story of the prodigal son, it's when he came to the end of himself that he started home. In David's story, it's when he takes ownership of his sin.

> *"For I know my wrongdoings, and my sin is constantly before me. Against You, You only, I have sinned and done what is evil in Your sight, so that You are justified when You speak and blameless when You judge."*
>
> *(Psalm 51:3-4)*

I did it, David confesses. *It was me.*

I'm not sure we can know exactly how David's sin transpired—not exactly. Whether he plotted and planned to take Bathsheba for months, or whether it was an impulsive reach to take her. Temptation itself is not a sin, but in David's case, the looking, the lingering, the longing, and the leaning toward sin drew him in.

Either way, David had rejected what he knew about right and wrong. He had rejected what he knew about God. He sat down on the throne of his own desires and sinned.

I can get away with this, David thought. And that was the affront to God.

To know God's character and still sin is grievous. John Bunyan, author of *The Pilgrim's Progress*, put it like this:

> *"Sin is the dare of God's justice, the rape of His mercy, the jeer of His patience, the slight of His power, and the contempt of His love."*

At the end of his sin, David was barely recognizable as *a man after God's heart*. If you allow sin to cause you to wander, it will make your life unrecognizable.

Still, God's mercy remains. And it's in that mercy that David placed his future.

3. When You Come Back to God, Hope in His Mercy

If you're looking for good news here, you've found it! God forgives sin! It's good news for kings and prodigals and everyone in between. All of us are sinners and desperately need the forgiveness of a merciful God. David set his eyes firmly on the forgiveness and joy that was slated for him:

> *"Purify me with hyssop, and I will be clean; Cleanse me, and I will be whiter than snow ... Hide Your face from my sins and wipe out all my guilty deeds ... Restore to me the joy of Your salvation." (Psalm 51:7, 9, 12)*

Amber, whose story opens this chapter, says about Psalm 51, "This is very real to me." This amazing possibility and promise has gripped people through the ages. Can this really be? Will God really cleanse me? The answer is very clear: yes. Yes, He will.

This is like the sunrise after a long night of anguish and pain. It's like the calm after the storm has swept through.

Amber's freedom from forgiveness gave her an entirely new frame for living. From the time Psalm 51 and forgiveness became real to her, she was able to put the shame of the past behind her, and live *out of* the forgiveness and cleansing that only God could give her.

David's prayer includes a series of statements that let us see what forgiveness really is. Forgiveness is not simply being sorry for sin or it's consequences. It's certainly not remorse from simply being caught or embarrassed by our actions. Forgiveness is also not just a wishful hope that God may forget it or let it drop.

No, forgiveness is the specific action of a holy God that puts away sin.

> ***"Purify me with hyssop,** and I will be clean." (v 7)*
>
> ***"Cleanse me,** and I will be whiter than snow." (v 7)*
>
> ***"Hide your face from my sins and wipe out all my guilty deeds."** (v 9)*
>
> ***"Create in me a clean heart, God, and renew a steadfast spirit within me."** (v 10)*

Do you see the instigator of the action? It's all God!

David is trusting and believing that God will act as only He can to restore David to a right standing before Him.

In this prayer, David is taken from one position (separation) to a completely different place (restoration) by God's actions. As painful as his previous condition was, the joy of restoration is even greater.

It's not that David's sin was without consequence. Even after David repented, he lost the son Bathsheba bore. That's another story altogether, but even the grief that sinful consequences bring us can be healed by knowing we're standing in His compassion and grace. It gives us the strength to trust Him for healing.

God *does* restore David to His grace and fellowship, and yes, He even restores him to be king. It's hard for us to get our head around just how big this restoration is that God gives.

God's is a radical and controversial love. There are some who believe God was overly gracious to David in restoring him as king, but that's part of the mystery and depth of grace. The older brother of the prodigal son was furious at the restoration of his wayward brother, but that's the kind of grace and forgiveness God shows. It doesn't always make human sense, but it's always welcome.

I, for one, am grateful.

As ever, the message of all Scripture points to the ultimate sacrifice made for the forgiveness of the sins of mankind.

David's forgiveness is a picture of Christ's forgiveness for all who put faith in Him.

Jesus actually came from the tribe of Judah and was a descendant of David when he came to earth to secure this kind of grace and forgiveness for the sins of the world! In dying on the cross, Jesus' death became the specific action of the holy God to put away sin. He is the only One we trust for this.

4. When You Come Back to God, Come Humbly

At the end of David's prayer, he makes one more statement that reveals his heart so well at this point. It's also a statement that can reveal our heart as well.

> *"For You do not delight in sacrifice, otherwise I would give it; You do not take pleasure in burnt offering. The sacrifices of God are a broken spirit; A broken and contrite heart, God, You will not despise."* (Psalm 51:16-17)

Psalm 51 is an invitation. It is a call to come back to God the way David came back.

Amber came to God, and her story is a constant reminder of God's great comfort and grace. She'll tell it to anyone who will listen: that God is able to restore.

Come, along with your sin and your broken heart, and you can be brought back to God.

Take your place in the long line of kings and prodigals and all of the rest of us who have learned to honestly and genuinely confess our sins and humbly receive His grace and forgiveness. Marvel with everyone else as you see God restore relationships, friendships, and opportunities to bring honor to Him instead of shame.

Each time I offer communion as a pastor, I take my congregation to 1 John 1:9 as a reminder of an unforgettable gift that God gives each of us. It says, "If we confess our sins, He is faithful and righteous so that He will forgive us our sins and cleanse us from all unrighteousness."

Sometimes I tell them to hurry to the throne of grace and get this cleansing. Life is just too brief and valuable to continue living far from the God who loves you.

Chapter 8

When God's Ways Seem Anything But Perfect

PETER'S STORY

"Simon, son of John, do you love Me?"

John 21:17

Peter is perhaps the most transparent of Jesus' twelve disciples. Because so much of his story is recorded in the Bible, we get unique glimpses into his struggles.

Nearly everyone can identify with him in some way. His was a life of the highest highs and the lowest lows. He was a bold follower of Jesus *and* a prolific blunderer. He spoke *up* for Jesus and *against* Jesus. Jesus loved him *and* rebuked him.

If you were to place Peter's life on a time line and chart his best and worst moments, you'd be sure to find a point at which you identify with him somewhere between those dots. Few have looked more brilliant and more reckless in the same period of time than Peter.

Just months after the mountain-top experience where Peter, along with two other disciples, witnessed the transfiguration of Jesus and the appearance of Moses and Elijah, Peter finds himself in an incredibly low valley.

After the Passover meal, when Jesus declares that "one of you will betray Me" (Mark 14:8), Peter responds with typical bravado, saying, "Even if they all fall away, yet I will not" (v 29).

Matthew's Gospel gives us a close and detailed view of what happens next. Almost immediately after Peter's declaration of loyalty, Jesus is betrayed by Judas, taken captive by the temple guards, tried by the Pharisees, and on His way to suffering and the cross. The disciples have largely scattered in fear, but Peter has stayed close, attempting to remain faithful. He's magnetically drawn to the surreal scene unfolding in front of him, hoping that all his hopes and dreams are not disintegrating. This is nothing like the future he has envisioned with Jesus.

As he watches, the hatred against Jesus intensifies, the accusations pile up, and the high priest tears his robes while accusing Jesus of blasphemy. This stirs the crowd to become a mob, bent on beating Jesus, spitting in his face, and slapping Him. Peter grows increasingly desperate. He's confused, afraid, and disillusioned.

Three times during this confusing scene, Peter is called out as an associate of Jesus, and three times, despite his previous bold claim to never leave Christ, Peter vigorously denies Him.

When it's over, Peter remembers the word which Jesus said:

> *"'Before a rooster crows, you will deny Me three times.' And [Peter] went out and wept bitterly."*
>
> *(Matthew 26:75)*

And there it is, for the entire world to see. Peter has denied Christ.

Even worse for him, the Gospel of Luke records one penetrating and often overlooked moment in that event.

"The Lord turned and looked at Peter." (Luke 22:61)

Can you imagine?

When Life Isn't What We Thought It Would Be

Before we count Peter out—before we criticize him for this cowardly moment—we ought to consider how common it is to do what Peter did. It's revealing to make an honest assessment of how many times we have been in the same situation in life.

Our faith in God is shaken because He's not doing what we thought He would. We see evil appear to triumph over good and believe that injustice has the final word. We give ourselves to faith and prayer, but it all seems futile. Our plans to build upon what we thought God wanted all fold, and heaven is silent. The marriage or family we thought God would give us has been deeply disappointing. Someone we trusted and believed in has fallen, and our confidence is shattered.

Somewhere in our grief and disappointment, we blame God. We wonder where He has been and why He allowed this to happen. God is not defending His character. He's not doing what we think a God like Him should do. And we *trusted* Him with our *lives!* This is unlike almost any other crisis of faith because God is not doing what we *know* He can do—and sometimes He is not doing what we *thought* He said He would do. It makes no sense at all to us.

If we have felt this way, we're not far from where Peter was that day. This is why disillusionment begins to creep into our minds and we loosen our grip on faith.

We might never say out loud, "I don't know the man," but we begin to act as though we would. We stop identifying with Jesus in the bold way we did before. And we know He sees us.

My wife, Kim, and I have been there. Years ago, my mother and father made the decision to move to the Dallas-Ft. Worth area, where we lived. For decades they had lived in the western part of the United States where they pastored churches, and visits were rare. It was my mother's life dream and dedicated prayer to live near her kids and grandkids. It was our prayer as well.

Mom had battled cancer in the years before moving, but it seemed to be in remission, and finally plans were made. Our kids were excited and eagerly anticipating their grandmother and grandfather being near. A home was secured within a mile of ours, and 15 years of plans and prayers were finally coming to pass. We were so eager to spend the years ahead together!

But two weeks after they moved, the cancer was back. Mom was hospitalized for exploratory surgery. We learned that the cancer was spreading, and despite our dreams and *seemingly* answered prayers, she died. She was so close to where she wanted to be but never experienced it.

It was a dark, disappointing, and disillusioning time for us. How could this happen? How could God allow the dreams and prayers of this amazingly selfless and deeply spiritual woman to be dashed against the rocks? How could He allow our kids this disappointment?

We knew all the spiritual and biblical answers, but at the time they didn't seem to help. We knew others were experiencing devastating trauma. We realized we were not the only ones who were experiencing a loss this overwhelming.

But this time it was us. Our faith was rocked, and we were struggling to trust God. He wasn't acting like the God we thought we knew.

For years, Kim had kept a small wooden block on a kitchen shelf with one of her favorite verses printed on it.

It was Psalm 18:30: "As for God, His way is perfect" (NIV).

In disillusionment and pain, she took that block off the shelf and threw it away.

God's way didn't seem so perfect during those days.

How do you come back from moments like that? How did Peter come back?

HE Is the Way Back

The answer to the question "How do you come back from moments like that?" is "You don't. Someone has to bring you back."

That someone is Jesus.

In the very last chapter of the book of the Gospel of John, we find a revealing conversation between Jesus and Peter around a campfire by the Sea of Galilee.

It's an interesting scene in so many ways. Jesus had died on the cross, and after three days in the tomb, was miraculously raised from the dead. He's appeared to the disciples, including Peter. In fact, Peter was among the first to see the empty tomb. In every plausible way, we think, Peter should be back on top of the world.

But he's not. Normally the leader and always outspoken, in the accounts of the brief post-resurrection period before Pentecost, Peter is strangely silent. He's been humbled, of course, by all that has transpired, but he's also struggling. We know this because John 21 recounts a conversation by the campfire.

Jesus appeared to the disciples eight days after the resurrection, and He's going to show Himself to them again at Pentecost, but Peter isn't aware of this. Things are different from before the crucifixion—exhilarating in some ways but different. Jesus is not physically present as often as before. He's alive, but what will come next is still so uncharted and uncertain to the disciples that they don't know what to do and think. So they do what comes naturally to them—what they used to do before.

Peter and six of the other disciples are together at the Sea of Galilee, and Peter says, "I am going fishing" (John 21:3). The others go with him.

The original language of Peter's statement suggests more than a fishing trip. It's more like *I'm going to go back to fishing. I'm going back to what I'm familiar with.*

And yet, after fishing all night, these veteran fishermen catch nothing. I'm not much of a fisherman, but I do know it requires a great deal of patience, and you often sit for hours in the night saying nothing and waiting for something to happen.

The next day, as the sun began to rise, something took place that changed everything for Peter and the disciples.

For just a few moments, I want you to imagine yourself in the boat with those disciples. You're disappointed, and even stunned, by the events you've experienced, and you're wondering about the future. Imagine you've been up all night doing what you used to do and not finding any reward in it.

Now look to the lakeshore, 100 yards away, and notice what John sees—a man standing there, calling out to you.

In Jesus' conversation with the disciples, He brings all of them (especially Peter) back from disillusionment and disappointment.

What Jesus does to help Peter, He can do for any of us.

He can help us put the pieces back together of dreams and expectations that have disintegrated. He is able to show us how the promises we held on to are not so empty after all, even though they appeared to be. He can help us trust Him again, and we will want to believe that He is not finished with us yet and be ready to get up and begin the journey with Him once more.

Remembering Who You Are

> *"Jesus said to them, 'Children, you do not have any fish to eat, do you?'" (John 21:5)*

I love how Jesus calls out to them. He calls them "children." It's an endearing term—a family term. It's the kind of word I've used over the years to address my own family—my own kids—and it says, *You belong to me. We're family.*

I recall being in deep and embarrassing trouble as a teenager, and my dad sitting me down and saying, "Listen, son. We're in this together. We're going to make this right." I knew in that moment who I was. I was my father's son, and I needed to hear that.

Of all the terms Jesus could have used, this one is the one He chose.

Jesus could have simply addressed them by name—or as a group of men.

Men, are you catching anything?

Instead, He calls them children. I'm sure they heard it—after all, they answered Him. Yet, it's clear they don't realize it's Jesus just yet. It's one of those surreal moments when someone is talking to you in a manner that only one other has spoken to you, and it brings back so many memories and thoughts—but you're not fully aware of who it is.

Just days before the crucifixion, as Jesus was sharing the Last Supper with His disciples and Peter was making his bold declarations of commitment, Jesus said, "Little children, I am still with you a little longer. You will look for Me ... where I am going, you cannot come." (John 13:33)

And now, after Peter's disillusionment, denial, and shame, he hears it again: "Children."

In the coming moments on the lakeshore, Peter would learn what we can know—that the relationship with

Jesus we have been given is filled with grace. It's unmerited and undeserved from the beginning, and it cannot be canceled by our failures. What Peter was before his denial, he still is—a friend of Jesus—in spite of everything. What grace!

The apostle Paul would later make this sort of family statement multiple times.

> *"For you have not received a spirit of slavery leading to fear again, but you have received a spirit of adoption as sons and daughters by which we cry out, 'Abba! Father!' The Spirit Himself testifies with our spirit that we are children of God, and if children, heirs also, heirs of God and fellow heirs with Christ."*
>
> *(Romans 8:15-17)*

> *"Therefore be imitators of God, as beloved children."*
>
> *(Ephesians 5:1)*

And of course, John, on the boat with Peter that day, heard it as well.

> *"But as many as received Him, to them He gave the right to become children of God, to those who believe in His name." (John 1:12)*

You, like the disciples, might not have realized that Jesus speaks to you that way, but He does. Jesus would remind you of who you are: a child of His. You're part of His family; you're a child of God. Even if you've been in disillusionment and heartbreak—you're still His child.

As an earthly father of six kids, I can imagine no possible scenario in which they are not my children anymore. How much more does our good heavenly Father consider us His children!

Remembering How to Trust Jesus Again

On that lakeshore, Jesus was helping His disciples remember how to trust Him.

> *"And He said to them, 'Cast the net on the right-hand side' ... So they cast." (John 21:6)*

It's mystifying to me that seasoned fishermen would have taken advice from someone standing on the lakeshore they didn't yet fully recognize—but, again, something powerful was unfolding.

It was at this moment that Jesus was taking them back to the beginning of their relationship, when He had taught them to trust Him the first time. Very early on, Luke records that as Jesus was beginning to teach by the lake of Gennesaret (Galilee), these fishermen listened to His teaching—and then heard Him tell them to go into deep water to let their nets down. Simon Peter, of course, said:

> *"Master, we worked hard all night and caught nothing, but I will do as You say and let down the nets."*
>
> *(Luke 5:5)*

They caught so many fish that the nets began to break. An unforgettable catch. An unforgettable lesson.

And the moment it was over, Luke tells us, they left everything to follow Jesus.

And, now, after the resurrection, Jesus does the same thing again.

Trust me once again, He says. They listen, they trust, and once again, they haul in such an incredible catch that they can't get it aboard.

It was at this precise moment that John said to Peter on the Sea of Galilee, "It is the Lord" (John 21:7).

The moment John recognized Jesus, it all came rushing back to the disciples. Their fears during Jesus' death had led to a failure to trust, and now they were reminded that they had every reason to trust again. After all, here He was!

Peter failed Christ because he allowed fear to dominate him. We have fears that dominate us—and threaten our trust of Christ, as well.

I fear being out of control of my life.

I fear trusting God and something not working out.

I fear what people will say if I follow Christ all the way.

I fear I won't enjoy life if I follow God.

I fear I will suffer something tragic and not understand.

I fear that what I believe about God and the Bible will be wrong.

I fear I will never be able to finish well.

I fear I won't be able to resist temptation.

I fear people will discover my flaws.

I fear that I will fail and God will not forgive me.

Jesus used a simple fishing illustration to teach His disciples that they could trust Him again. He's always reminding us that He can be trusted in everything, but we only learn it when we obey. For example, Jesus was reminding the disciples to trust Him when the storm came up while they were in the little boat. "'Why are you afraid, you men of little faith?' Then He got up and rebuked the winds and the sea, and it became perfectly calm" (Matthew 8:26). There was the moment on the hillside with 5,000 hungry people and very, very little food, when Jesus said to those same disciples, "You give them something to eat!" (Matthew 14:16). Of course, He shows them how this all works when they bring the five loaves and two fish to Him, and He blesses and breaks them in the supernatural way He does things, and everyone ends up full.

Trust Me enough to obey Me, Jesus says.

Jesus knows fishing better than the disciples. He knows relationships better than we do. He knows marriage, parenting, business, friendships, and life better than we do. And, importantly, He knows *us* better than we do. Learn to trust Him again.

When my middle daughter was a teenager, she and I attended a father/daughter camp high in the Shasta Mountains of California. It was an incredible camp and a beautiful experience in those mountains that summer.

One day, while we were riding horses together across huge green pastures, I watched her saddle begin to slip to the side, and soon she tumbled to the ground. At first I was alarmed due to the speed of the horse and the impact as my daughter fell, but then relieved to see she was unharmed.

The rider leading the group told her, "You must get back on the horse again. If you don't, you'll never regain the confidence to ride again." It was good advice, and we took it. After securing the saddle, I boosted her back up, and we had an amazing ride together. It's still an incredible and lasting memory. She has never regretted getting back on that horse.

Sometimes, you just have to get back in the saddle and learn to trust again.

Remembering How to Love Jesus Again

In that moment in John 21 when Jesus is on the lakeshore, there is the unusual scene where Peter leaps out of the boat when he realizes that it is Jesus calling to them. At first this sounds wildly impulsive, and so much like the Peter we've come to know in the Gospels. But the more I deliberate on and soak in this scene, the more I realize that Peter is simply overwhelmed by all Jesus has done in these moments to restore him from disillusionment, denial, and distance. He has bridged the gap, and Peter knows it.

Jesus has reminded them all of the original moments when they first began to love and follow Him. He's reminded them that He called them children before by still calling them children now. He's reminded them that He's still the Lord of the winds, waves, and seas. He taught them so much on those little boats over the three years when they were following Him. And He's reminding them of it all now.

When it all comes rushing back into Peter's heart—that Jesus is still the same Jesus and is still inviting Peter to follow Him—Peter simply cannot wait another moment to obey that call, so he deliberately dives into that lake to get to Jesus first.

What a moment!

It's that moment that leads to the unusual conversation Jesus has with Peter, all alone.

> *"Simon, son of John, do you love Me more than these? ... Tend my lambs." (John 21:15)*

Do you love Me more than your boats and your fishing? Do you love Me more than your friends? Do you love Me more than comfort and familiarity and safety? Do you love Me more than these?

Countless messages have been preached about these words, utilizing every nuance of the language. But they should never obscure the primary reason for the conversation.

Peter, can you learn to love Me again?

I'd like to believe that by that point Peter had recognized the love that Jesus had for *him*—that he had witnessed Jesus' definition of love, recorded in John 15:13:

> *"Greater love has no one than this, that a person will lay down his life for His friends."*

Peter had seen that take place. There could be little doubt of Jesus' love. It's so much easier for us to love Him when we realize that we've been loved this way *by* Him.

In the end, love for us found in Jesus and our love for Him will overtake any expectations we have of what He might do with our circumstances or with His honor and glory. He doesn't need us to direct Him or defend Him. He just wants us to follow Him. We learn to lovingly yield to however He leads.

There are times when Jesus calls us to isolate ourselves with Him and we are all alone in His presence. Or you know God is at work when it seems like no one else is in the room—it's just you and the Lord. These times are special, and at times like these, His incomparable love becomes very real to you.

Do you allow yourself to have those moments? I would plead with you to never miss those moments with God. They may be uncomfortable, even difficult, but they are powerful.

Do you think Peter wept that day on the lakeshore? I think he did. He wept bitterly when he realized he'd betrayed Jesus. I believe he wept again before Jesus on that lakeshore, but this time in gratitude for the grace and love and acceptance he had experienced that morning.

At the end of it all, Jesus called Peter back to the beginning.

"Follow Me!" (21:19)

Follow Me to the end, Jesus says to Peter.

It was about a year after our disillusionment with my mother's death that my wife, Kim, found another wooden block—almost exactly like the one she'd thrown away—

and painted those same words on it again, in trembling faith. It still sits on her dresser.

"As for God, His way is perfect." (Psalm 18:30, NIV)

By His grace, we're going to live the rest of our lives embracing that truth.

And so can you.

Chapter 9

When God Takes Us to the Brink

HEZEKIAH'S STORY

"In those days Hezekiah became mortally ill."

2 Kings 20:1

My wife and I were sitting across the table from the "Bosom Buddies." These four women were friends from our church, and I'd heard portions of their stories several times in my years there. I knew they regularly gathered to talk about their journey. They wear the term Bosom Buddies proudly, and they should; they are quite the team.

These ladies know well the shock, the fear, and the loneliness of battling life-threatening illness. For them it was breast cancer. This night, we had the privilege of hearing them speak first-hand about coming back from their physical crises. Two of them are fifteen years beyond their original diagnosis, and two are eight years beyond that challenging season of their lives.

Each had faced the crisis with faith. Each had reached out to others. Each had come back from cancer and was sharing how that challenge had changed their life and faith. Every story had common threads—threads that bound them together with God and with each other. As they talked, they smiled—glowed even—with the countenance of people who have been given "bonus years."

They also wanted others to know what they had learned about God in the valley of the shadow of death. Somehow, speaking with them and learning the secrets they had discovered in that season brought a measure of peace and confidence to my own heart. We never know when we will find ourselves in such a valley—and it is hard to know how to prepare.

But *they* knew. The Bosom Buddies also freely talked about the character that was shaped through the physical challenges they faced during that time.

The Dark Valley of Life and Death

Hezekiah was in this kind of valley. The "valley of the shadow of death" is actually King David's line. It's in the familiar "shepherd's psalm": Psalm 23. The valley of the shadow of death is not necessarily the place where you die, but it's a place where death is so close, so threateningly real, that its shadow passes over you.

> *"Even though I walk through the valley of the shadow of death, I fear no evil, for You are with me." (Psalm 23:4)*

It doesn't matter who you are: the shadow of death is always close because death is all around us. We're constantly reminded of it, and there is no safe place from its reality. You've been there if your health has been threatened, if you've narrowly avoided a tragic accident, or even if someone close to you has lost their life. That shadow has us all in some way.

For most of us, death is not forecast with a date and a time stamp on it, but for King Hezekiah it was. In the middle of a long and faithful reign, this great leader of Israel became mortally ill. Isaiah the prophet was sent by God to Hezekiah with this message:

> *"This is what the LORD says: 'Set your house in order, for you are going to die and not live.'" (2 Kings 20:1)*

With that statement, Hezekiah was immediately in crisis mode.

In the considerable number of passages detailing King Hezekiah's reign, this pronouncement comes out of nowhere. He was a good leader. He made bold and courageous moves that repositioned Israel in the favor of God—favor that had been lost in the reign of his father, King Ahaz.

Hezekiah came to the throne at the age of 25 and immediately drew closer to God. He "did what was right in the sight of the LORD" (2 Kings 18:3). A summary of his reign includes removing the high places of pagan worship, breaking into pieces a bronze serpent that the people had begun to worship in place of God, and generally repositioning the nation's faith back in God. 2 Kings 18 says it plainly:

> *"He trusted in the LORD, the God of Israel; and after him there was no one like him among all the kings of Judah, nor among those who came before him." (18:5)*

The pronouncement of his impending death comes as a complete surprise. There are no signs that God is disciplining him or exposing hidden sin in Hezekiah. He's not under God's judgment. In fact, God is *using* Hezekiah and the nation to discipline Sennacherib of Assyria and remove his presence from the land. It is just after a military victory—won because an angel of the Lord appeared and slew 185,000 Assyrians in the night—that Hezekiah gets his bad news.

The timing of this pronouncement helps form our theology of suffering. Physical crisis, in the form of a terminal prognosis, is most often not the fault of the suffering one. It doesn't necessarily happen because of disobedience in our lives. God is not out to get us, though we may wonder that when bad news about our future emerges. At times, physical crisis takes place in order to *test* us—uncomplicated by any other reason.

Because these things are true, it doesn't make sense for us to seek out the "why" of these moments, as we're all prone to do. It does, however, make sense to treat these seasons as a time in which to trust God and allow the test to shape us in the best possible ways.

This was the *test* of a lifetime for Hezekiah. How he faced it, and who he became on the other side of this illness, is the *lesson* of a lifetime for us. As Hezekiah begins his desperate personal journey of praying and pleading with God, there are few surprises. At the end of the journey, though, is an ending that no one anticipated.

What to Do in the Valley

How did Hezekiah respond to his crisis? How should we respond to ours?

1. Focus on God. The text wastes no words. The shift from pronouncement to prayer is instantaneous, according to the text.

> *"Then he turned his face to the wall and prayed to the LORD." (2 Kings 20:2)*

Hezekiah has honored God in his life and in his reign. He has been a good king in so many ways, but now he's been given a terminal prognosis, and he is reeling badly, as any of us would be.

Bad things sometimes happen to good people who obey God. This is difficult to understand or reconcile ourselves to, but it's true, and Hezekiah knew he had to face the wall and focus on God. Looking anywhere else would have been futile. We can't know exactly why he faced the wall, but we can conclude that facing the wall probably kept him from looking elsewhere for help and kept others from distracting him. This was, at the very minimum, an extremely focused prayer.

When a prophet like Isaiah proclaimed a prophecy, it was as good as done. This is not a conditional pronouncement. It's not a doctor's opinion or a paranoid thought. Hezekiah hears it as fact and knows there is no way to minimize the weight of this.

He is appropriately desperate. If you've been there, you know what's next.

Hezekiah is getting *focused* on God, and he's getting *personal* with God. No doubt he has questions, as we would, as this pronouncement hits him between the eyes. He may have been struggling with his fears, anger, or disappointment. He may have raised his voice in protest or disbelief to God. We can't be sure, but it's a relief to know that God never penalizes us for that. It becomes obvious as this scene unfolds that Hezekiah does nothing to displease God in how he is seeking Him.

God gives grace in those moments when He allows a crisis.

When I was talking with the ladies who'd gone through breast cancer, they expressed a wide range of responses to their crisis: from a calm surrender to whatever God might allow to a stunned and surreal feeling of disbelief. One of them immediately began to think through the insurance coverage and family details that would need to be discussed.

No matter what the individual response was, God extended the grace and space needed for them to process the crisis. He never left them. He never shut them down. He was there.

2. Evaluate Your Life. Hezekiah's prayer as he faced that wall was brief but profound. It was deeply personal and emotional. He weighed his life before the Lord.

> *"'Please, LORD, just remember how I have walked before You wholeheartedly and in truth, and have done what is good in Your sight!' And Hezekiah wept profusely."*
>
> *(2 Kings 20:3)*

Desperation should make us evaluate. Nehemiah was desperate when he heard about the condition of Jerusalem during the exile, and his desperation made him honestly consider the state of the entire nation before he prayed, "Lord, may Your ear be attentive to the prayer of Your servant" (Nehemiah 1:11).

Desperation made another king of Judah, Jehoshaphat, think about where exactly things stood when he prayed, "For we are powerless ... nor do we know what to do, but our eyes are on You" (2 Chronicles 20:12). *We're not looking anywhere else, Lord!*

For Hezekiah, desperation leads him to remember his life of faithfulness. He is looking for reasons for God to spare him. He's reluctant to die, feeling the same way that most of us would. Maybe he's concerned about family, the nation, or his responsibilities.

When crises happened in the past, where was Hezekiah? He was the one to intercede for the nation. He saw God rescue His people by sending an angel in the night to slay those 185,000 Assyrians in the camp. Hezekiah's prayer must have brought back these memories.

Desperation also makes us remember God. Remember how you sought God when a crisis hit in your past. Remember how the character and the ability of God was demonstrated in that time. Remember how He answered those prayers.

I remember several years ago reading a magazine article by Kenneth Doke about counseling individuals through life-threatening crisis. He recalled a counselor telling him that she could predict the way he would approach his death—namely, the same way he responded to any other life crisis.

There's truth here. Don't for a moment believe that God has not prepared you for crisis moments like these. He may well remind you of that when you face them.

3. Reckon with Your Empty Feelings.

"And Hezekiah wept profusely." (2 Kings 20:3)

What does this mean? Simply that this bitter weeping revealed the emptiness of the king. He was completely, totally emptied. He had no resources with which to rescue himself, and there were no healers to intervene. It was he and God alone.

Hezekiah's prayer was amazingly brief. Less than two dozen words are uttered before he broke down weeping. It's been said that sometimes weeping is the best kind of praying because God understands the language of tears.

It's not the length of a prayer but the depth of surrender that God is looking for. Prayer may be difficult, but surrender is *more* difficult.

Sometimes we have no idea at all of how to pray. Those are the times when even our groans and sounds of weeping are translated perfectly in the heart of our God.

The apostle Paul, writing about praying in seasons when we don't know what words to use, says, "In the same way the Spirit also helps our weakness; for we do not know what to pray for as we should, but the Spirit Himself intercedes for us with groanings too deep for words; and He who searches the hearts knows what the mind of the Spirit is, because He intercedes for the saints according to the will of God" (Romans 8:26-27).

I'm so grateful to know this. When we're empty, He hears our prayers.

It's a desperate place, but it's the best place to be when in crisis.

Corrie ten Boom, a survivor of Nazi concentration camps in the Second World War, said:

> *"The wonderful thing about praying is that you leave a world of not being able to do something, and enter God's realm where everything is possible ... Nothing is too great for His almighty power. Nothing is too small for His love." (I Stand at the Door and Knock, p 63)*

Hezekiah prays and surrenders.

And then something amazing happens:

> *"And even before Isaiah had left the middle courtyard, the word of the LORD came to him, saying, 'Return and say to Hezekiah the leader of My people, "This is what the LORD, the God of your father David says: 'I have heard your prayer, I have seen your tears; behold, I am going to heal you. On the third day you shall go up to the house of the LORD. And I will add fifteen years to your life.'"'"*
>
> *(2 Kings 20:4-6)*

I love these pivotal moments in stories and in Scripture. Throughout the Bible, we read verses that describe desperate moments met with divine interventions. God graciously and immediately answers Hezekiah's prayer in a way that he could not have imagined.

As good as this news is, there are questions in our minds. Why does God declare one thing but do another here in this story? How does God act sovereignly but change course in response to a prayer? How does all this work together?

Could it be that our desperate moments are divinely orchestrated to drive us closer to God? Could they be tests of our faith? Could they be the foundations on which we learn to deny panic, set aside the fear and anguish that we first feel, and hold on to the answers God gives us instead of our assumptions?

Remember a man named Job? Remember desperate moments in your life when you were pressed to really, truly, and deeply cast yourself on Him?

Have you read the book of James lately? "Consider it all joy, my brothers and sisters, when you encounter various trials, knowing that the testing of your faith produces endurance" (James 1:2-3).

One of the Bosom Buddies said about the verse above, "That was my verse from the beginning."

Some of the greatest moments of my life have been my most desperate ones.

The ladies at our table talking about their cancer spoke of the challenging crossroads of faith where they were asked to think and trust God like never before.

"I was told to choose joy."

"I determined to let it make me better, not bitter."

"I was afraid but grateful for His presence."

"God told me, 'I've got this.' I chose to believe Him."

God was working to develop their characters during this season. Joy instead of anguish. Optimism instead of pessimism and gloom. Gratitude instead of fear.

To a person, the Bosom Buddies glow with faith and confidence in the God they love. They've been desperate—and have had to trust. They've seen God meet them in that dark valley.

And for them at least, God has brought them out of cancer to the other side in this world.

I know it doesn't always happen this way, and it's important to acknowledge that a physical crisis such as this sometimes ends in death. Many are not healed of sickness in this life who have prayed just as hard and trusted just as deeply.

I watched my own mother lose her battle with cancer when I was convinced we had prayed just as Hezekiah did and when there were so many more things she wanted and felt she needed to do on earth.

I don't have all the answers, but I do know God's grace and goodness met my mother and our family in those hours, and though she is dead, her influence lives on.

The more I live life, the more I see people walking with invisible pain and difficulties, while being buoyed by the persistent grace God gives them.

But when God *does* allow us to come back from a physical crisis, what is He giving us a chance to do? Why is He giving us more time? Isn't there a significant purpose for what we see as our bonus years?

Learn the Lesson of the Valley

Surprisingly, Hezekiah failed to answer these questions, and this is where the entire story of this great leader turns downward.

> *"But Hezekiah did nothing in return for the benefit he received, because his heart was proud."*
>
> *(2 Chronicles 32:25)*

His pride and arrogance during the years God gave him brought judgment upon the nation in the next generation, and nearly all he had worked for in his lifetime was lost.

His failure stands as a *lesson* to us that God has a reason for our time on earth and we should seek that out. He gives grace and strength—and importantly, the right kind of perspective to live a life that will honor Him!

It's up to us to grasp the life God is giving us day by day. If we could only live our life with as much desperation for purpose as we have for health!

Which brings me back to our friends around the table.

Like Hezekiah, they reached out to God in desperation. Like him, they were spared and given more time. Unlike him, they found the humility and gratitude for meaningful and fruitful life on the other side of the dark valley.

Life now, for them, includes a *deeper level of trust* in God.

> *"Trust in the LORD with all your heart and do not lean on your own understanding. In all your ways acknowledge Him, and He will make your paths straight."*
>
> *(Proverbs 3:5-6)*

It takes a great deal to trust God with your health and future, but a crisis can help get you there if you are willing. We can get to that place of trust that Paul describes, knowing "that God causes all things to work together for good to those who love God, to those who are called according to His purpose" (Romans 8:28).

We may not be able to *explain* how things work together for good, but we come to know that they *do* in His hands. No one could convince me otherwise.

Life in the valley for these ladies *brought a kinship with others* as they walked through their challenges. The community of faith become more visible, more powerful and more real. Each spoke of the powerful effect of praying people in their lives. For them, compassion and sympathy for others in the valley of the shadow of death became a defining quality in their prayer lives and ministries.

All of them minister to others going through similar seasons. One wrote a book; another is a gifted teacher who keeps their stories of grace going. They are *using* this season in which God has met them.

After the battle with cancer, *trivial things became trivial again*. After all, what mere nuisance can really get our attention when we've been facing down life-or-death crises? Priorities became more clearly defined, and things that were small and inconsequential just didn't get space in their minds or conversations. They live much more focused lives now.

"Life is too short to hold grudges," one of the ladies said. "I just don't do that now."

Finally, life on the other side of critical illness involves *a new sense of gratitude and worship*.

"I'll never worship the same way," said one. "Every moment is a gift."

I've watched these people on a regular basis. Their joy is unmatched—and contagious. They've learned the secret of gratitude that few know.

Life in this world is not ultimate. Because of the resurrection of Jesus Christ, and the promise of heaven, we know about a future hope that is glorious. On the other side of this life is a greater existence than anything we've known here, but that future is shaped by what we do with our time on earth now.

To be aware of the brevity and value of life is priceless.

Perhaps the greatest prayer to pray is this one:

"So teach us to number our days, that we may present to You a heart of wisdom." (Psalm 90:12)

Chapter 10

What God Began, He Will Complete

YOUR STORY

"For I am confident of this very thing, that He who began a good work among you will complete it by the day of Christ Jesus."

Philippians 1:6

In the introduction of this book, I promised real-life scenarios that would give us hope. The stories you've read highlight various ways in which God brings us from defeat to victory.

This final chapter is about your story—your own situation and season of life. It may be the most important—and memorable—chapter of the book. It's about your personal journey.

I frequently tell my own story. When I was 6 years old, I became gravely ill and had a high fever for an extended period of time. One of my earliest memories is one of my parents holding me in a bathtub filled with water and ice in an attempt to break the fever. I didn't understand at all what was happening. Their desperate faces and my confusion as to what was happening are still vivid in my mind.

That night, the fever broke, and I began to recover, but as a result of the fever, I lost my hearing through inner-ear nerve damage in both ears. The loss of more than 90% of my hearing in both ears meant that my world went largely silent. I could only hear sounds that were accompanied by strong vibrations, such as the slamming of a door nearby or a heavy bass beat in music. As a young boy, my world became one of silent moving lips and actions that had no sounds. I felt alone and separated from everything around me. I could not even hear my own voice.

My amazing parents jumped into efforts to alleviate the problems of my silent world, which included lip-reading classes, hearing aids, and thinking through every possible way to help me function in a hearing world. Elementary teachers in my small town joined the army of helpers, and I honestly believe this team of incredible people made my world so much better than it otherwise would have been.

But life was still difficult, and the challenges were endless. Plus, I had some weighty questions about it all. *Why is everyone else normal while I have this hearing loss? Where was God when this happened? How can a God who is supposed to be able do anything sit idly by when I'm struggling badly?*

I was convinced that life was unfair and that I was a victim.

I can't remember how many times God reminded me, *I'm not done with you yet. The story is not over. Why can't you trust Me for the next chapter?*

Slowly, I learned to trust Him for one thing and then another. And now I trust Him daily. He's still not done! My journey of faith continues, and I'm in no way disappointed with what He is doing!

It's inevitable when we read the stories of people who have encountered God's help and grace that we compare our lives with theirs. While our experiences will not all be the same, the One who is working in our lives is the very same One who worked in the life of Moses or Abigail or Joseph.

What If You Stop Believing?

When we consider the lives of those we've read about in this book, we should ask, "What would these people have been like if they had never listened to God or been open to His help? How would their stories have been different?" It's not difficult to imagine how quickly Jonah would have perished in the deep. It doesn't require much thought to realize how David's kingdom could have completely unraveled, or how bad the situation could have been for the Jews if Esther had not trusted God.

But there are many stories in the Bible and in our lives of those who did *not* allow God to bring them back. I know some of those stories as well. I've helped counsel people when life went from bad to worse because someone close to them refused to consider that God was not through working in their lives yet.

I frequently think about where I would be today if I were "on my own." I don't like what I envision. In fact, one of the saddest things in life is watching people stop short of allowing God to fulfill His purpose and promises in them. He's simply never done until He calls us home.

As I've written this book, my prayer has been that God will shine the spotlight on and in your lives—and with it, I've prayed that He will help each of you to believe that His grace is available.

Have you wondered if God was done with you? Have you stopped entertaining the "what if" question that God sometimes surprises us with? "*What if* God were to do this work in my life or answer this prayer? *What if* He were to give me next steps in the days ahead." I hope you can anticipate exciting new parts of your journey.

What to Remember When You Resume the Journey

When God calls you to get back on the road of life with Him, you need reminders of His ways and to be challenged with a few questions.

Try these:

- Are you running *to* God or *away* from Him?
- Are you *winning* or *losing* the battle against the world, the flesh, and the devil?
- Are you *transparent* with your life, or are you *hiding* what you've done or how you've lived?
- Have you *settled* the past, or do you *struggle* with all that you've experienced?
- Are you at *peace* with God, or are you *angry* at Him?

These are a few questions we must ask to begin a journey back to spiritual health.

These next statements will remind you of what you need to know about God as you consider a comeback season in your life.

Reminder #1: God is completely aware of where you are and what is taking place.

Sometimes this truth is uncomfortable, especially when we prefer things to be hidden. At other times, this is the most welcome truth in the world. I may feel lost, but God knows where I am!

David reminds me of this often in the Psalms. "Where can I go from Your Spirit? Or where can I flee from Your presence? If I ascend to heaven, You are there; If I make my bed in Sheol, behold, You are there" (Psalm 139:7-8).

This truth helps me know I don't have to get God's attention. He's already aware.

When we experience loss and grief, we can expect to be met at the same time with a wave of God's grace. Instead of looking for God, know that God is here for us in the worst moments of our lives. God is aware.

Reminder #2: You're never alone. God is there. He is with you. This is generally true in that God is omnipresent. He's literally everywhere. It's also specifically and practically true for every believer in Jesus Christ. The promise of salvation for those who trust in Christ's death on the cross and surrender to Him as Lord is the promise of the Holy Spirit.

The Holy Spirit indwells each believer, and He is always with us. This means you're never truly alone when you think you are, and it means you don't have to reach far to come back to God. He's been there all along.

Even in the Old Testament era, God demonstrated that He was with those who needed Him. The greatest description of Joseph's life in prison was that "the LORD was with him" (Genesis 39:23).

As though that were not enough, He specifically declares He is there:

> *"For He Himself has said, 'I will never desert you, Nor will I ever abandon you.'"* (Hebrews 13:5)

Reminder #3: God still keeps His promises.
Some of the greatest stories in the Bible involve promises from God to His people, which He kept, no matter how impossible the circumstances were. God's promises still apply to His people today, and He is still the promise-keeping God.

The Bible is filled with promises that God made to others in the past and has made to us as present followers of Christ. He will help us discover, remember and trust in these promises as we search for them.

I settled my own issues with God over my hearing loss when I read the passage where God told the apostle Paul that he would be given enough strength to overcome every physical and spiritual difficulty. I read this during a time when I was doubting my ability to obey God in what I sensed He was calling me to do. I was willing, but I knew my limitations. Then I read this promise:

> *"And He has said to me, 'My grace is sufficient for you, for power is perfected in weakness.' Most gladly, therefore, I will rather boast about my weaknesses, so that the power of Christ may dwell in me."*
>
> *(2 Corinthians 12:9)*

The promise God gave Paul became mine by application. God is the same unchanging God, and as followers of Christ, we are His people as much as Paul was. I've learned in the decades since applying that verse to my life that God keeps His promises well. His grace *is* sufficient.

What promises of God are you holding on to?

Reminder #4: God's resources are endless.

The wisdom displayed by Abigail and Esther in trying moments is impressive. Where did they get it from? From God! God gives amazing insight, strength or resolve—and he sends others to encourage us or counsel us just when the need is the greatest.

James 1:5 might well be the verse of Scripture I quote most often. I need it constantly.

> *"But if any of you lacks wisdom, let him ask of God, who gives to all generously and without reproach, and it will be given to him."*

I'm convinced we miss many of the resources God sends our way because we forget where they are or who He uses to convey them—or we simply fail to ask for them.

How can you find the truths and wisdom you need without the Bible? How will you have life-changing conversations if you're not part of the body of Christ—the church? They are "your people" when times are difficult. Where do you get your counsel? Be sure it comes from people of the book—the Bible.

God speaks through His book and His people. He gives these resources and more.

Reminder #5: Patiently waiting for God to speak or act keeps us from self-destructing.

Moses' anger and impulsiveness set him back instead of moving him forward. If he'd only waited for God to work, his life would have been far simpler! That's true of us too.

Joseph in prison is a textbook example of patient endurance. Instead of organizing a prison protest, he waited on the God who never forgot him. He kept himself from self-destructing and when the time was right, God elevated him to power.

David needed Abigail to *keep him* from self-destructing. Unknowingly, he was possibly about to forfeit his future kingdom—but God used Abigail to help him be restrained. Most often, we do not need to take matters into our own hands; we need to trust Him.

Reminder #6: Grace and grit work well together.

We can't do anything well without God's grace, but He also calls us to endurance. There's a line of advice I've given to people over and over through the years of leading and counseling. Early on, I thought it was a shallow piece of counsel, but I now know it has tremendous value.

"Hang in there." It sounds shallow, but it's actually deep. And it's biblical.

It's important to hang in there while waiting on God to

work. We hang in there when marriage is challenging or when raising kids is making us crazy. Those seasons will pass if we don't give up. We have to hang in there when life feels awful, knowing it will change at some point. We must hang in there, because the opposite is to give up.

And why would we want to give up on our important journey toward eternity?! Amazing things—and people—are awaiting us! "Therefore, since we have so great a cloud of witnesses surrounding us, let us also lay aside every encumbrance and the sin which so easily entangles us, and let us run with endurance the race set before us, fixing our eyes on Jesus, the author and perfecter of faith, who for the joy set before Him endured the cross, despising the shame and has sat down at the right hand of the throne of God" (Hebrews 12:1-2). I can't remember the number of times I've needed to see that Jesus saw joy *beyond* the cross which kept him going *through* the cross. That same joy can keep us going, too?

To say "Hang in there" is to say, "Live life with endurance—with grit." And ultimately, it is God who gives us that grit. A favorite verse for me is this one:

> *"But by the grace of God I am what I am, and His grace toward me did not prove vain; but I labored even more than all of them, yet not I, but the grace of God with me."*
> *(1 Corinthians 15:10)*

That's grace and grit.

Reminder #7: During every difficult season, God is building us to become more like Christ.

If we remember that God is always at work to help us become more like Christ, then this reminder is a welcome one.

This is the reason why my friends, the Bosom Buddies,

said they can rejoice in their battles with cancer. They knew God was using those difficult seasons to do a work within them, even as their bodies were in pain.

I'm encouraged by every part of Romans 8. These verses are particularly important:

> *"And we know that God causes all things to work together for good to those who love God, to those who are called according to His purpose. For those whom He foreknew, He also predestined to become conformed to the image of His Son, so that He would be the firstborn among many brothers and sisters." (Romans 8:28-29)*

He's shaping us, and knowing that He is using our circumstances to cause us to be more like Christ is a great encouragement.

Basketball was my favorite sport in high school. My junior season was unforgettable in my memory, and the guys on that team all feel the same way.

We were not a good team in the first half of the year. By the Christmas break we'd lost twice as many games as we'd won. No one was talking about playoffs—or state championships.

No one, that is, except our coach, Gary Looper.

I remember a meeting we had in our gym where he had us all sit in the bleachers while he stood in front of us, outlining the Christmas-break practice schedule. Instead of a break, it sounded like boot camp. It felt like it too.

We looked at each other in disbelief. *We* were done. But *he* wasn't done with us yet. He was right, of course. The season wasn't over though, we felt it was.

What Coach Looper did for us that day was remind us that he believed in us and he had a plan that would result in a comeback season. All we had to do was follow the plan. He knew our team. He knew our potential and the opponents we'd face, and he said he believed we could change the course of our season.

We worked hard (a definite understatement) during the break and resumed play. If memory serves me well, we won 15 of the next 16 games, and came up through a tough bracket to win the state championship tournament.

Most of us would say that our season turned that day in the bleachers, when the coach told us what we could accomplish. To this day, it was one of the greatest coaching moments I know about.

We still had to work, to sweat, and to grind it out, without a doubt. And I want to give credit to the key players on that team, who played such great ball and won that championship.

But the truth is, someone had gone before us to chart the course and had called us to it.

Someone has gone before you to chart the course of life and is calling you to it.

How will you respond?

thegoodbook
COMPANY

BIBLICAL | RELEVANT | ACCESSIBLE

At The Good Book Company, we are dedicated to helping Christians and local churches grow. We believe that God's growth process always starts with hearing clearly what he has said to us through his timeless word—the Bible.

Ever since we opened our doors in 1991, we have been striving to produce Bible-based resources that bring glory to God. We have grown to become an international provider of user-friendly resources to the Christian community, with believers of all backgrounds and denominations using our books, Bible studies, devotionals, evangelistic resources, and DVD-based courses.

We want to equip ordinary Christians to live for Christ day by day, and churches to grow in their knowledge of God, their love for one another, and the effectiveness of their outreach.

Call us for a discussion of your needs or visit one of our local websites for more information on the resources and services we provide.

Your friends at The Good Book Company